Energy 4 Life

High Energy, Conscious Living

Energy 4 Life

High Energy, Conscious Living

Caroline Shola Arewa

THIRD EYE

Energy 4 Life: High Energy, Conscious Living
/ *Caroline Shola Arewa*

ISBN - 978-81-8274-516-2

First Indian Edition: 2011

Original English edition published by O book (imprint of John Hunt Publishing Ltd.) UK. India Edition published arrangement by Pentagon Press.

First Published in India by

THIRD EYE
An Imprint of
PENTAGON PRESS
206, Peacock Lane, Shahpur Jat,
New Delhi- 110049
Phones: 011- 64706243, 26491568
Telefax: 011- 26490600
email: rajan@pentagonpress.in
website: www.pentagonpress.in

Printed by
Syndicate Binders
A-20, Hosiery Complex, Phase- II, Noida-201305

This edition is for sale in indian Subcontinent only.

CONTENTS

Dedication vii

Acknowledgements viii

Introducing Energy 4 Life 1

Chapter 1 Energy, Vitality and Conscious Living 6

Chapter 2 New Look at the Ancient Chakra System 25

Chapter 3 Science and Spirituality - Quantum Divine Mix 44

Chapter 4 Energy and Ecstasy - the Power of Sacred Union 58

Living Consciously in the 21st Century 75

Chapter 5 Energy Exercises – Honouring your Physical Temple 78

Chapter 6 Energy Psychology – Values, Beliefs and Lifescripts 99

Chapter 7 Energy Food – Rainbow Diet 119

Chapter 8 Energy Balance – Relaxation and Meditation 138

Chapter 9 Energy 4 Life Coaching – Transforming the way you Live 158

Glossary 176

References 179

About the Author 182

Resources 183

Personal Notes 184

Dedicated to

Spiritual revolutionaries and seekers everywhere

"I'm starting with the man in the mirror. I'm asking him to change his ways.
And no message could have been any clearer,
If you wanna make the world
a better place, take a look at yourself,
and then make a change."
Michael Jackson from Man in the Mirror

Acknowledgements

I give thanks and praise to the Creator, the most high. I thank my Ancestors for continued protection and guidance. Love and thanks to my family and friends for lasting love and support.

Colleagues, mentors and clients all over the globe who have supported my work over the years, too many to mention individually, I love and thank you. All who have attended Energy 4 Life trainings, workshops and individual sessions; you have helped me develop this work and allowed me to be on purpose in my life. I appreciate and give thanks for you all.

Special thanks to Tony Pinfold for the cover image, Alvin Kofi for the illustrations, Belinda Mollross, Stephen Tallett PhD, Julia Akintunji, Anne-Marie Newland, Sankofa Mustapha thank you all for your love and support. Susan Mears, John Hunt and the publishing team at O Books, thank you for supporting me in many ways that have made this book possible.

For all those not mentioned, who have taught me, influenced me and walked with me on this journey of life. I am eternally grateful.

Introducing Energy 4 Life

Energy, Consciousness and Change

- Would you like more **Energy and vitality?**
- Do you want to raise your **Consciousness and quality of life?**
- Are you ready for **Change**?

Yes! Then Energy 4 Life is for you.

Most people want enough energy and vitality to live life to the full. We don't want to feel drained, exhausted and stressed out all the time. And why should we when being full of energy is our birthright. Energy is the fuel humans are designed to function on. We need regularly topped up, good quality energy for optimum health and wellbeing.

Yet work pressures, relationship issues, parenting, financial worries and fears for the future, all drain energy and create stress. Stress leaves us feeling tired, wound up and low in energy. In our fast paced I need it yesterday world. The only constant is change. And when everything changes we must adopt new coping mechanisms.

How you manage personal energy is the new key to raising consciousness and creating a high quality of life.

Energy is the fundamental building block of life. Energy is motion, vibration, the very life force that animates and moves through us. Energy is life itself.

Everyone is familiar with energy and we describe energy in different ways. How many times have you said or heard others say *'I feel full of energy'* or *'I am low in energy'*? Have you heard people speak of *being in good spirits or* having *no energy left at all?* We speak of liking and disliking other people's energy or vibration. Energy is very much part of our experience and common language.

My research and work over the past 25 years has people calling me the Energy Doctor. I have practiced energy medicine, holistic healthcare, humanistic psychology and ancient spiritual traditions. I have studied quantum physics, new paradigm medicine and consciousness studies. I've travelled worldwide and experienced how people maintain their health and achieve success in many different cultures.

This led me to develop a powerful, culturally diverse, energy-based approach to conscious living I have taken the most potent, quick acting, easy to use techniques for elevating energy and created Energy 4 Life.

Energy 4 Life – E4L – is a natural healthcare system and conscious living programme that activates and elevates your core energy. It works with the chakras and human energy system (HES) because underlying everything in life is the flow of energy.

This powerful energetic approach raises consciousness and coaches you to live a healthy, happy and successful life in the midst of our changing world.

E4L simply asks two questions:

How do you use or abuse your energy?

How could you use it better?

When you allow energy to flow freely in infinite supply your life is enhanced. Flow of energy in the human body, mind and spirit is the foundation of health and success. Therefore E4L encourages energy flow by using an integral approach of four modalities that re-align, re-vitalise and increase energy flow; each one is based on a different element.

Energy Exercises (Earth) Specific stretches and yoga postures designed to develop physical health increase body awareness and enhance your overall flow of energy.

Energy Psychology (Air) Thought power, energy economy, release technique and mind processes are all taught, as they offer potential for deep and lasting change.

Energy Foods (Fire) The energetics of food are explored with the aim of restoring nutritional health. This includes water cleansing and the healing power of eating raw and living foods.

Energy Balance (Water) Relaxation and meditation tools that instantly affect your nervous system inducing self-regulation, healing and higher consciousness. Energy Balance reduces your body's stress chemicals, balances emotions and promotes energy flow.

E4L draws on ancient spiritual teachings and the cutting edge sciences of quantum physics, neuro-biology and consciousness studies. It is a meeting of science and spirit that beautifully answers the calling of our time. This programme goes beyond enhancing health and utilises coaching skills to support conscious living and help you get from where you are to where you want to be in your life.

How to use this Book

So you are ready for change, ready to embrace E4L. This book offers easy to use tools and techniques as well as energy theory. So you can make practical changes in your life and elevate your energy and consciousness.

I have worked with thousands of people worldwide and I've seen lives transformed as a result of applying simple techniques.

Something as seemingly basic as drinking two litres of water a day can transform your health forever. A simple alignment technique can totally re-balance and uplift your system. And learning to breathe fully and use the amazing power of your mind offers you infinite potential.

This easy to use book will benefit you in so many ways if you are:

- Well and want to maintain your health and energy levels
- Healing and want to restore your energy for health and wellbeing
- Making life changes and want to uplift your energy
- On a spiritual journey and want to raise your level of consciousness
- Ready to enhance your life embracing more health, happiness and success

Read the book anyway you will. Front to back, back to front, dip into it, write in it, reflect on it and do the exercises from it. Make notes in it or in your journal. Listen to your subtle energy and create lasting change. Enjoy it, tell your friends about it. Gift them with it.

Get all up in it and embrace all the energy you desire for your life. There is no shortage of life energy, it is available in abundant supply.

I offer Action Programmes in chapter nine so you can incorporate E4L everyday, creating dharma, a way of life. This book also accompanies the popular Energy 4 Life workshops and Practitioner/Coach Training. This book presents a conscious living programme. It provides the opportunity for you to elevate energy, raise consciousness and embrace change. So enjoy reading and allow yourself to step into the infinite potential and greatness unfolding in your life at this wonder-filled time.

Wishing you abundant Energy 4 Life

June 2009

Chapter One

Energy, Vitality and Conscious Living

'I merely took the energy it takes to pout and wrote some blues'
Duke Ellington

Energy

What is Energy?

Everything is energy. Energy is the fundamental building block of life. It is the animating life force manifesting through, around and as you.

You are pure vibrant energy. Einstein's famous equation $E=mc^2$ [1] tells us that everything animate and inanimate is made from pulsing creative energy. It is everywhere in all things in the tiniest subatomic particle, the breath you breathe and the solid ground on which you stand. It's all vibrating energy. Energy is the container, the carrier of in-form-ation, the intelligent force through which all things come into being. Energy manifests in the physical, emotional and spiritual aspects of your being. It is expressed through all things in all densities.

As energy we are part of an evolutionary journey of consciousness. Out of the void of nothingness came all things. Like the great oak emerges from the acorn. The Ancients speak of ether or akasha, which scientists call the quantum vacuum both referring to the empty space of infinite possibility from which all life emerges. This potential space of consciousness, energy and in-form-ation shapes itself into what we know as matter. Waves, particles and light become the living world we see around us. The same energy surrounds, permeates and is who you are. You are energy. Energy, consciousness and information manifesting as *You!*

Energy is also the fuel you are designed to function on. It is the power that manifests in both subtle and gross form. Your body, thoughts, emotions are all pulsing, vibrating energy. The food you eat, the space between each breath, the paper you are reading, the chair you are sitting on and the ground on which you walk. It's all energy, there isn't anything else; everything is energy.

> *"Leading-edge research is suggesting that the so-called "empty space" within and between atoms is not empty space at all; it's so lively with energy that one cubic centimetre, a thimbleful, a marble size, contains more energy than all the solid matter in the entire known universe"*
>
> Will Arnzt

Hand Energy Sensing

Let's explore this with a simple yet powerful exercise I use in my workshops. It helps you get a felt sense of energy. Sit comfortably either cross-legged on the floor or if that is difficult, sit upright in a chair with both feet flat on the floor. Straighten your spine, this allows your chakras to sit on top of each other in vertical alignment.

Place your hands, palms facing upwards on your knees. Close your eyes and take a few deep breaths. Let your body relax. Remain upright releasing any tightness. Relax your shoulders and let them open. Expand your chest, lift your spine and take up more space in your body. Now bring your attention to the point just below your navel; feel the sensation of energy or visualise a healing colour. Slowly draw energy up from below your navel through the abdomen and chest. Feel the energy move and direct it around each of your shoulders and along your arms to your hands.

Be still and sense the energy in your hands. When you feel a sensation in your hands, lift them up from your knees and turn them to face each other. Begin to bring your hands very slowly together sensing the energy. Explore the space between your hands. The more subtle and imperceptible you move the more powerful is the feeling of energy. Draw your hands slowly together until they touch. Then gradually return your hands to your knees. Take a few deep breaths and remain with your eyes closed for a moment.

Through this exercise you can feel the energy that permeates and surrounds you. You experience the minor chakras and electro-magnetic field around your body. You may feel heat, tingling or excitation. As you draw your hands together you may encounter a resistance, a sense of something solid amidst your hands.

If nothing is felt during the first few times you practice Hand Energy Sensing, don't give up. It may just be that your concentration needs to be a little more focused on sensing. Possibly you moved your hands too far, too fast. Continue practicing this exercise to develop your awareness of energy.

I trust you now have an intellectual idea and a felt sense of what energy is. You are infinite energy, filled with the possibility and potential to consciously shape the world in which you live.

Where does Energy come from?

We know when we are feeling drained. We have a good sense of what and who drains our energy. We know when we are low in energy, off colour, as we sometimes call it. We also realise that we need energy for optimum health. Being full of energy, vibrant and animated is highly desirable.

We all want more of it so we can do the things we love. I haven't met anyone yet who doesn't want to experience life fully. And most of us want to live life to the max!

I began this chapter with one of my favourite quotes; it seems Duke Ellington learnt to master his energy. So where does energy come from?

In physics the concept of energy is defined as *a quantifiable attribute of physical systems*[2]. I refer to energy as a building block. Energy can neither be created nor destroyed. It can however be transformed from one form to another. The food you eat transforms into your body's nutrition. The Duke's pout was transformed into blues.

Energy comes in many forms from the subtle force we know as vital energy or prana to the solidity of your physical body and the material universe. Like water which forms steam, fluid and ice, energy can manifest in different densities.

There is gross physical energy, emotions, thoughts are subtler and subtler still is high frequency spiritual energy. These are all powerful forces that you can learn to manage efficiently to achieve an improved quality of life.

All actions in life require energy. It is the power behind reaching your potential and being in your greatness. E4L has energy at its core because energy fuels health, happiness and success. Ancient wisdom and modern science agree that everything, including you, is made of energy. Energy is known by many names, such as prana, chi, shekem, asè and vitality. The Ancients had a developed understanding of the Human Energy System (HES) and mapped its existence both in and around the body.

Energy is my passion and area of expertise, particularly the HES and the chakras, which are subtle energy centres in your body, with direct links to the neuro-endocrine system. The chakra system is like the hardware on your computer. If it goes wrong the software can't run. Likewise, when your chakras are out of balance your life can't run well. Chakras are the energetic core of your existence. They are power stations, responsible for generating and distributing energy throughout your body. Energy flows through a series of pathways known as nadis or meridians and like electricity it is an invisible force.

As to where it comes from; to the Ancients, energy is a gift from the gods. It is everywhere and in all things. It comes from the sun, the waves, the earth and the winds, all forces that power us. And in science it's much the same, energy has many sources heat from the sun, fuel from the earth, power from water and wind. We have been blessed with an abundance of energy. Our task is to learn to use our energy resources effectively.

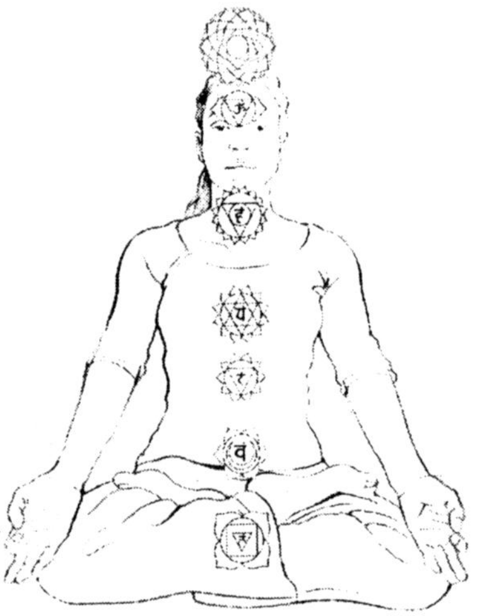

The Seven main Chakras

How Effectively do you use your Energy?

When energy is depleted and out of balance you can experience tiredness, fatigue, stress and dis-ease. Learning to balance energy effectively creates the health, happiness and success we desire. Knowledge of energy, chakras and the HES enhances spiritual, personal and professional development. The more you understand energy, the more successfully you can manage your life. Energy is the key to a high quality of life.

We naturally attempt to measure our energy levels:

Energy	Measurement Scale
1. Spiritual	flowing or blocked
2. Psychological	positive or negative
3. Emotional	good or bad
4. Physical	high or low

High energy living depends on you optimising all available energy. As complex energy beings it benefits us to draw on all our energy resources and not simply drain our physical capacity. It is vital to allow spiritual, psychological and emotional energies to work towards your success. How do you use or abuse your energy resources?

Let me break it down a bit. The overall energy available to you is 100% as your energy resource; 25% is available in each of the four areas spiritual energy, psychological energy, emotional energy and physical energy. How do you use or abuse each of these aspects of your energy? For example do you overuse your physical resources, using 60% from the 25% of physical energy available to you, causing depletion, stress and exhaustion. Do you only use 5% of your spiritual energy leaving 20% untapped potential and a sense of emptiness instead of fulfilment?

I ask these question to many clients and receive a variety of answers. Many people fail to use their spiritual intelligence, emotional intelligence and thought power, instead they rely on physical effort to achieve results. Invariably this leads to overwork, stress and exhaustion. We are multifaceted human beings designed to utilize all our resources and function on all the capacities of our body, mind spirit and emotions.

Getting to grips with how you use and abuse energy is essential for healthy and successful living. Taking time to understand your energy system allows you to take greater control of your life. It's all about operating from your core energy to raise your level of vitality and transform the way you live.

How did you answer the question, did you identify areas where you use excessive energy? Do you have unused resources and areas that require more attention; spiritual energy maybe? Could you use your energy in a more balanced way? Take time to answer these questions in your journal.

How can you get more Energy?

Despite the ever changing, fast moving, pressure filled 21st Century we live in; it is possible to have abundant energy and live without stress, exhaustion and burn out. This can be achieved by embracing a process that helps you transform the way you look at life. It is important to recognise that *life is all about energy and how you manage it.* When you make this paradigm shift and learn skills for managing energy – your vital life force, you will always have all the energy you need for life.

In today's world of rapid change and uncertainty we have to learn fast or risk being left behind. Many people manage time and stress with limited amounts of success because the real issue is how we manage personal energy. E4L gets to the core and simplifies life by helping you manage your energy resources. I refer to this as Energy Economy.

Why do some people live high-energy lives while others suffer constant energy shortage? Energy is life's primary building block and balanced living is dependent on effectively managing personal energy. E4L reveals the secret by introducing four modalities for energy management.

1. Energy Exercises increase the quantity of your energy – high/low
2. Energy Psychology improves the quality of your energy – positive /negative
3. Energy Foods raise the vibration of your energy – high/low
4. Energy Balance elevates the frequency of your energy – elevated/depressed

E4L aims to enhance energy flow and improve the quality of your life. These four modalities impact every area of life, elevating your ultimate life force.

So many people face health problems, harbour emotional wounds, suffer the pain of relationships, career challenges and money worries. This all causes energy depletion and stress. Focussing on energy directs us to the very heart of our existence and provides a simple alternative to how we view and cope with life. How are you using your energy and how could you use it better, becomes the main question? This is a paradigm shift, a new way of looking at life's many ups and downs.

The solutions E4L offers stand the test of time. Tools are embraced from the East and West as well as from ancient and contemporary practices that can help you re-fuel, find inner stability and create personal balance in this fast changing world.

High-energy people, exude vitality, passion and enthusiasm, all ingredients required for success. To have more energy you need to raise awareness of these four vital areas and live consciously.

Managing Energy

I draw on yogic philosophy, humanistic psychology and my experience of consciously managing my own energy and working from an energetic perspective with clients. I bring this knowledge together in an accessible model called E4L, which provides a unique synergy of spirituality, holistic healthcare and personal development. E4L is a system that can be used simply and quickly to get positive and lasting shifts in your energy levels without years of study. E4L is a powerful solution for health, happiness and success.

Life constantly presents shifts and challenges. But as you learn to manage personal energy you gain inner balance and stability in the midst of change. Balance is not a destination but a journey and E4L assists you as you travel. It is a road map for life, helping you successfully increase and manage your energy, vitality and well-being.

In the first part of this book you learn about energy and its many principles. It is essential to have a good understanding of what energy actually is and how to cultivate and elevate energy in order to manage it better.

Sexual energy is one of our most powerful energies and possibly the most misunderstood. We see it flaunted in advertising, we see it used to abuse and control people, it's feared, suppressed and made shameful. There are all manner of dysfunctional attitudes to this potent drive. When sexual energy is understood as a powerful creative force moving through all of us, it creates the possibility for this force to be harnessed and expressed positively.

E4L explains how this power can be used to prevent illness, improve health and ignite creativity, passion and vitality.

The second part of this book moves on to explore the practicalities of energy management. It details how this approach can be used to create high energy conscious living. I share information from ancient and contemporary approaches to energy psychology and energy balance. Timeless wisdom and modern science both contribute to our understanding of managing energy.

The real meaning of balance is explored, plus tools for creating it. As you get familiar with core energy and its management, you begin to recognise what enhances and zaps your energy. I share the five main reasons we get low and fatigued and share some powerful two-minute techniques for recharging your inner battery and staying on top in times of stress and overwhelm.

A lot of work has been done recently to educate people about diet and nutrition. Food is energy. E4L brings to light the unconscious processes behind food choice. This helps you understand the energy of food enabling you to make better choices.

We are complex beings with a multitude of needs that nurture body, mind and spirit. Yet when we choose to look underneath the complexity and identify what is really required for our health and well-being, we see that it is simply energy. We need regularly topped up, good quality energy for optimum health and wellbeing.

Can you see the pattern I'm building and the simplicity that underlies it? When we adopt this new paradigm of energy management things become surprisingly simple. How are you using your energy and how could you use it better? This is all you need ask in relation to any area of your life. Be it health, relationships, creativity, happiness, success or even time because energy is the underlying principle.

Energy management offers a powerful new way of organising our lives and attaining balance and fulfilment.

Creating EASE

Let's use the example of a busy professional for a moment – a man works long hours, gets little time off and takes insufficient rest. He realizes it is causing stress and disruption to his family life, but he just doesn't know what else to do. He needs to support his family that means keeping his job, which means accepting the unspoken *overwork* ethic. This is a common situation many of my clients find themselves in.

Ok, so think energy. How is he using his energy and how could he use it better?

First of all in energy terms *less is more*; long hours working hard with little rest is not an efficient way to use energy. It is exhausting and it doesn't produce the best work. It impacts on his family, causing energy drain on them as well as himself. He thinks he is supporting his family, so probably resents the lack of appreciation he gets at home. He's reluctant to challenge the overwork culture so he is holding back what he really feels at work. In energy terms this is a disaster waiting to happen; high blood pressure, a heart attack, immune disorders, maybe a divorce. Unfortunately this scenario has become normal but it fails to be natural. We are human beings not human doings.

So what can be done energy-wise? Looking at this in energy terms forces us to look at the big picture. It begs us to prioritise in order of importance. This will be very similar for all of us. Although often taken for granted when we assess the big picture health, comes up top of the list. Without health the quality of life can be seriously impaired. We all value the ability to take care of our own basics like feeding and washing ourselves. The ability to enjoy life fully is reduced when health is impaired. Therefore most of us recognize its importance. Family and friends come next, the need to love and be loved to share life with significant others. And finally expression through work, that allows us to earn. Yet energy tends to go out in the opposite order. Most going into work, next family and friends and little into personal health.

Just seeing the picture differently already creates an energetic shift. We see that more time needs to be spent on personal health and with family members and less time at work. To achieve this, a more efficient way of working needs to be established. I can hear people saying, 'but the job still needs to get done' and that is true, but it can be done more efficiently.

E4L introduces energy economy. Rest and relaxation at home and work are vital for getting more done in less time. The brain works more efficiently when we rest and use whole brain technology, instead of forcing the mind. Spending time with loved ones is a double energy boost. You feel good and so do they. This supports health and wellbeing all round. It's all about transforming the way you live and creating ease in life Energy, Awareness, Success and Excellence.[1] When you are not creating ease in your life you are creating dis-ease. Whether it's in your body, home or workplace learning to manage energy creates EASE.

Vitality

There are numerous ways to bring balance and vitality to your energy system and assessing the use and abuse of your energy resources is a good way to begin. As long as you are alive energy is flowing through your system. Chakras are always open and therefore you are already working with your energy anatomy. Your vitality is determined by how much energy is flowing through you and the degree to which your chakras are open.

Throughout time it has been recognized that to obtain more from the universe we need to be open to receive more. Implementing energy exercises, rest and relaxation into your day along with positive thoughts and actions opens you to more energy. This increases your level of wellness and fulfilment in life.

When insufficient energy is flowing through your body physical ailments can occur. Although energy is quantifiable it remains elusive. For this reason we tend to speak about energy in our bodies using metaphor.

Metaphor is the Language of Energy

People can be heard saying:

I feel as if I have the weight of the world on my shoulders

She is a right pain in the neck

Head over heels

I can't stand it anymore

I feel as if I have been kicked in the stomach

I am afraid and have knots in my stomach

I am heart broken

I feel a bit off colour

I feel very down

I can't see the point any more

I am sick and tired of everything

He used to light up my life

I feel held back

These are just some expressions used to describe feelings and emotions when energy flow is restricted. These common expressions actually describe energetic qualities and how they affect our vitality. The flow of energy is disturbed by how we feel and that is described in these popular sayings. Energy is low, held back, broken at the heart, lacking direction. The language of energy allows us to better communicate what is happening inside. After all E-motions are simply Movements of Energy. Our emotions have a direct impact on our energy levels.

What affects our Vitality and Energy Levels?

Emotions, events, people and environments all affect our vitality and energy levels. Your experiences leave lasting imprints on your energy field. Trauma, for example, can drain energy creating depression and withdrawal. The body and energy field contract in response to trauma in an attempt to prevent energy drain or what is also called leakage. Chronic contraction interrupts full expansion and disturbs the natural rhythm needed to maintain health.

Pleasure and love have an expansive effect on the energy field, which can help repair some of the damage caused by trauma. Everything we do has a consequence on the energy field. Diet, lifestyle and the company we keep all cause vibrations throughout our energy system.

Thoughts have a considerable impact on your energy. 'Energy follows thought' is one of the basic laws of nature. Through your thoughts you are capable of changing your life. Therefore, you must be vigilant and think with awareness. A negative belief can manifest just as easily as an affirmative thought. The universe supports "My life will never change," just as easily as "things are going to improve for me." The choice is yours. As humans we are gifted with a high level of consciousness, so we can make choices.

People we spend time with affect us energetically. Some people leave us feeling tired and drained, while others help us to feel uplifted and joyful. We all know situations where someone entered our space feeling down and giving off negative vibrations, if we are not careful, we also begin to feel the same negativity. We need to be vigilant about the company we keep and aware of the vibrations we want to maintain.

We can feel our energy lowered in certain places where the energetic frequency is low. Likewise energy can be lifted in certain environments. We often experience a sense of expansion when we leave the city and visit the countryside. This is why people enjoy spending time by the sea or up in the mountains. People take pleasure from being in open spaces because the energy field is allowed to expand. This is also the reason for needing to get outside after being in a building all-day or going to the countryside after being in the city for a while. Your energy field actually requires more space. The energy field is very subtle, but by improving your awareness it is possible to interact more consciously with your energy on a daily basis and as a result improve the quality of your life.

Energy field awareness

This is an invitation to develop your conscious awareness of energy fields. For the next few days pay attention to your own vibrations and the energy fields of those around you. Fully use your senses, feel, look and tune into vibrations. Watch how you respond to certain people and them to you.

Observe:

- Your family at different times of the day
- People in your workplace
- How people interact on public transport
- Children, lovers, colleagues
  Notice how they move in and out of each other's auric space
- What it is about people that attracts you and draws you

close?
- What makes you pull away from people?

See if you can sense:
- A calm aura
- An agitated aura

Really attempt to sense the energy field, see its colour, shape and density. Make some notes in your journal and see if any recurrent patterns become apparent.

When I do this I seldom see colours. Instead I notice the size and energetic quality of the energy field. Some people's energy is so dense that it is hard for them to hold the attention of one person. Another character can hold the attention of many individuals around them because people feel embraced by their energy. For example, the pure energy of babies and small children has an amazing ability to attract and uplift people.

What uplifts your energy? What experiences, people and places bring you most happiness and fuel your energy? Heightening your awareness of energy improves wellbeing, raises your vitality and supports you to live life more consciously.

Conscious Living

Wellbeing is dependent on the harmonious flow of energy. E4L is more than a book, it is a complete natural healthcare system that can change your life and help you coach others to do the same. It's a coaching programme based on the ancient chakra system that utilises exercise, psychology, diet and relaxation to create more vitality, health and success. It's all about conscious living.

Living consciously asks us to step up our intentions and attention. It requires us to take responsibility for our health. It re-introduces simple teachings that can be shared with our families. The advent of 20th Century living created very dependent lifestyles; people depend on cars and seldom walk therefore more exercise is needed for vitality. Technology dominates our lives with television and the media influencing how we think. Our minds need to be cleared through relaxation and meditation. Foods became processed and available 'conveniently' no growing or preparation required. No waiting needed. This removed us from nature and the rhythms of life. People used to witness autumn when things rest' before blossoming again in springtime. Preparing food was a slow nourishing process. Our lack of attention and consciousness has caused us to strip our lives of energy without seeing the long term impact. Which is stress, exhaustion and fatigue caused by our 24/7 lifestyles.

Rest is essential to growth. E4L supports you to create energetic and conscious changes that bring greater physical health, psycho-emotional stability and spiritual awareness. Each modality in E4L is based on one of the four elements: earth, water, fire and air. This helps us re-connect with the energising rhythms of nature

The Elements of Life

The HES is closely associated with the elements; this has a history going back to Africa and the first people who walked on our planet. They lived at the mercy of the elements and were familiar with the overwhelming force the elements had on their existence. Energy has the power to both create and destroy; storms can destroy just as the sun creates. The elemental rhythms of nature bring creation, growth and destruction. This close relationship with nature and the elements made people aware of forces within the body as well as surrounding them. They began to liken the mind to the wind, forever changing, creative yet elusive. Over thousands of years a complex system developed which relates the elements to human experience. This legacy remains in popular metaphor today. We still refer to people as full of hot air, down to earth, a bit wet or too fiery.

This enduring wisdom, sometimes considered primitive, is a timeless science. The Ancients both understood and acknowledged the importance of energy. They realized that energy unites all things and affects us in positive and negative ways.

Modern science is just beginning to accept that all things are connected. Einstein's equation $E=mc^2$, informs us that what we think of as matter, is actually energy in a constant state of change and motion.

Entanglement theory in quantum physics, suggests that all things are connected and constantly interacting. The Ancients appear to have known this. Additionally, they realized their own energetic nature could affect people and the environment. This is called the observer effect in physics. As we study the elements and the HES we gain a deeper knowledge of our essence and begin to recognise ourselves as microcosms within the macrocosm.

Every person's energy signature is unique. And each one of us has a role to play in the greater scheme of things. We have a divine purpose, a mission to fulfil a contract to keep. This mission requires authenticity and connection with your unique personal qualities. We are all born with divine gifts. Talents to share with those we meet on life's journey. As you walk successfully through life sharing your divine gifts with others, you help them achieve their own divine purpose. Like a jigsaw puzzle where every piece counts toward the success of the whole. If just one piece is missing the entire puzzle will never be complete.

Lasting Success

The Ancients can teach us a lot about success. I am sure we all agree that success equals power. That is part of its attraction. The Ancients realised that real power is lasting. It is not something that can easily be removed. The sun cannot be taken out of the sky, just as the wind cannot be tamed.

A president however, can be brought down and voted out. Wealth can be lost, material goods extinguished by fire,

Hollywood or the CEO of your company can elevate you one day and send you crashing down to earth the next.

Power, dependant on external circumstances is limited power. Inner power based on alignment with the elements and forces of the universe is infinite power. Honouring your authenticity and the wholeness of your being, following your soul purpose and being true to your Divine inner-sense creates lasting success.

Spiritual energy or inner power is vital to lasting success. Success is often viewed in a very limited way. When we define ourselves as successful according to status, financial wealth and the accumulation of material goods we are standing on very shaky ground. The feelings of success generated by the above can be removed very quickly because they are based on impermanence. Achieving success on this level is merely part of the journey, the changeable aspect. We all know from observation or experience that money, status and material goods can bring comfort but not lasting happiness and fulfilment.

In energy terms they provide the foundation on which to grow, when we have them we can progress on to more meaningful things in life. We need food, shelter and comfort. We also need relationships and to feel powerful in our homes and communities, but beyond this we need to satisfy an inner longing for meaning and purpose in life.

I have seen a steady increase of progressive souls opting for more meaningful lifestyles. Lifestyles that take the planet, its wildlife and its people far and wide into account; ecological living, recycling, buying fair-trade, supporting causes concerned with the elimination of poverty, making small moves towards global change, even voting in Obama, a US President who stands for positive change.

More and more people are choosing lifestyles that favour personal health and not just company wealth. Talk of work/life balance, emotional intelligence, family values and personal leadership are all commonplace. This shift demonstrates a greater awareness of self and highlights the fact that we do have choices and we can be responsible for our actions and the impact they have on both our immediate environment and the world at large. This is conscious living.

This shift leads me to believe we are taking part in a spiritual revolution, a transformation of consciousness. The threat of the unknown is a wakeup call inviting us to transform ourselves and in so doing enhance our world. Many people are now answering this calling. As the human potential movement, once the domain of the enlightened few, expands and matures we are seeing people willing to take responsibility for their lives and the environment we live in. Many of us are willing to make changes, willing to *be the change* a spiritual revolution calls for. We are part of a revolution, a movement of rapid change and rotation that is taking us back to review the ways of old.

We are evolving spiritually and changing the world in which we live. We have the opportunity, more now than ever, to tap into a vast reservoir of spiritual intelligence. This powerful resource can help us re-design our lives. It can support us in developing greater compassion and love for all humans and other life forms. I believe we are welcoming in, what I call, an age of unity consciousness; a shift to heart-centered living through heart chakra energy.

E4L is a meeting of science and spirit that beautifully answers the calling of our time. According to both systems everything is energy. Tapping your core energy raises consciousness, generating knowledge and wisdom. It develops meaning, purpose and lasting success. It connects you with the infinite source of your being. Successfully managing personal energy is the new paradigm for creating health, happiness and totally transforming your life.

Chapter Two

A New Look at the Ancient Chakra System

"The Human Energy System provides a map for your most important journey, life. Its seven fuel stations/chakras represent a full range of human experience and possibility. Taking you from fear to faith, rage to radiance and vision to manifestation."

Shola Arewa

We are standing at the crossroads of major transformation. Our planet is crying out in pain as the mighty winds of change blow up a powerful storm. Our world is in the midst of so much chaos and confusion. And one of the major issues people complain of is lack of energy.

The Energy Crisis we are currently facing is not limited to our environment and the planet we live on. The crisis extends to each one of us, and the bodies we live in. 21st Century living is literally bringing us to our knees. These challenging times cause us to dig deep in search of answers. As we seek solutions we must come face to face with the part we each play in this global turbulence.

An effective resolution requires us to get to the very core, and the core is *energy*. This can be a turning point. We hold the potential and the opportunity to create meaningful and lasting change. The Ghanaian concept of Sankofa recognizes the need to look back in order to move forward. In these difficult times we must look back, as we need as much wisdom as we can get to propel us forward. As Einstein said *"No problem can be solved from the same level of consciousness that created it."*

We must remember that the future is not a definite reality that awaits us. It is for us to consciously create the future together.

The 21st Century, the much awaited Age of Aquarius, offers a chance for transformation. This is an opportunity to elevate our consciousness.

So how do we elevate consciousness? I believe it is time to take a new look at the ancient chakra system. Much of my work over the past two and a half decades has focussed on the ancient chakra system.

I have traced knowledge of the chakras back to the Mount Meru in Africa, close to the birthplace of humankind. The peak of the mountain represents the Crown chakra and its base the Root chakra. Here people lived honouring the earth and all the elements.

The elements have a profound effect on us, body, mind and spirit. We are made of the elements, earth being the solid physical body, water the ebb and flow of our emotions, fire our potential for rapid transformation as seen in the fiery digestive system, and air the elusive changeable nature of the mind. The elemental rhythm of life brings creation, growth and destruction. This trinity is seen in all life forms as the cycle of birth, life and death. Each chakra relates to a different element and stage of life.

Chakra is a Sanskrit word describing wheels of consciousness that are thought to be responsible for generating, transforming and distributing energy. According to the Ancients, chakras form the central energetic core of our existence. The HES provides a map for the important journey of life.

Seven main chakras represent a full range of human experience and possibility. They transport us from the personal and material realms through the dynamics of interpersonal relations to the transpersonal realm of the Divine. The chakras offer an ascending ladder of personal, psych-emotional and spiritual development. As we ascend we go on a journey which embraces multiple intelligences, IQ or rational intelligence, EQ or emotional intelligence, and SQ or spiritual intelligence. It's a sojourn inviting us to expand into our infinite potential. This journey takes us from Embodiment to Enlightenment and beyond. The ancient chakra eystem incorporates so much that I consider it to be an original Theory of Everything.

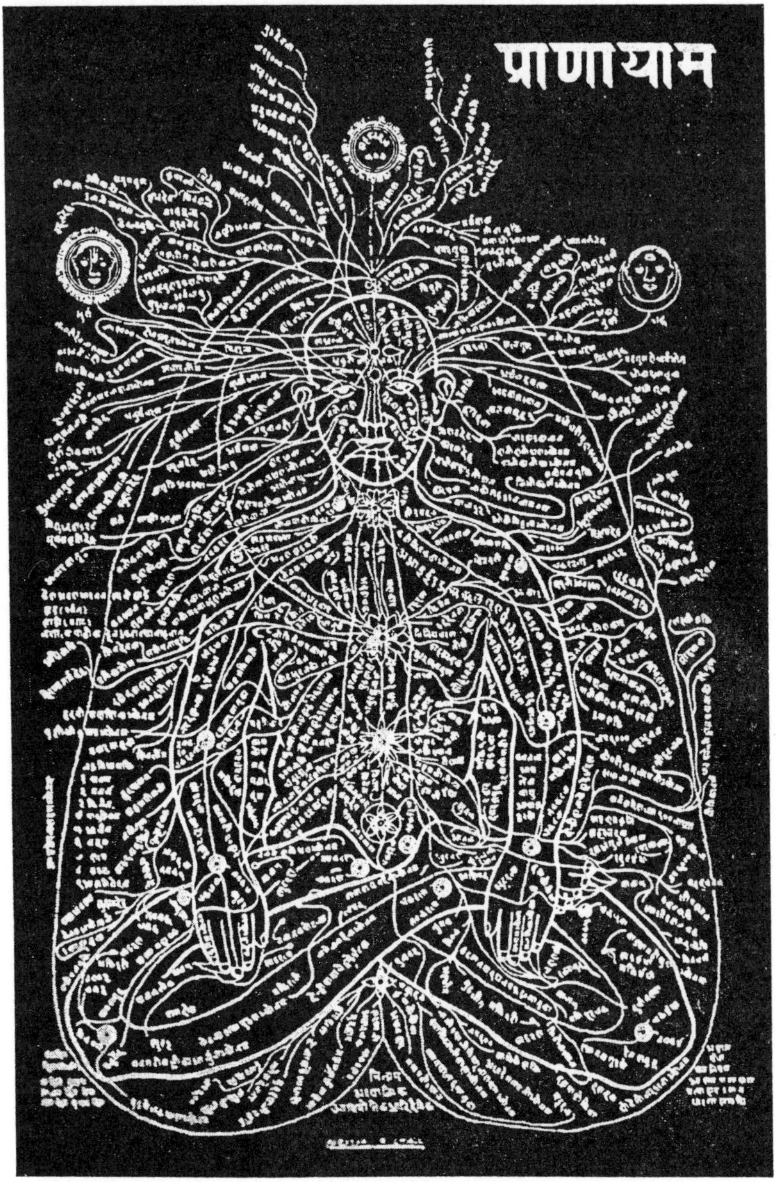

Human Energy System - Chakras, Nadis and Aura

Chakras are like power stations generating energy for everything we think, feel and do. If you want to improve the quality of your life and enhance your level of success, then chakras hold the key. Through understanding the chakra system, you can elevate consciousness and transform your life.

The seven main chakras of the ancient system are situated along your spine; the first chakra is at the base of the spine and the seventh is at the crown of your head. The image above shows the human energy system, consisting of energy centres along the middle, energy pathways, known as meridians or nadis, and the subtle energy field that radiates out from your body. Chakras are at the heart of the HES and they form a major part of your spiritual anatomy. These wheels of life set everything in motion.

Chakras provide an organizing principle, a metaphor of life, all things can be seen, understood and organized in relation to where energy is expressed or repressed in the chakra system. Each chakra governs a different aspect of your life and its development. The Ancients depicted their knowledge of chakras as spiralling energy mandalas. We all know a picture paints a thousand words, so mandalas which are sacred symmetrical images, allow a large amount of information to be portrayed about life and its infinite potential.

Tapping into energy and the chakras helps you understand your development and ascension of consciousness. This integral system provides insight into your physical health, psycho-emotional stability and spiritual evolution. The subtle vibrational frequencies of the HES integrate the old with the new. Chakras unite spirit and science bringing together the Newtonian mechanistic *believe it when you see it* worldview with the newer quantum physics *see it when you believe it* worldview.

Chakras support involution and bringing dreams into reality by birthing them in the world. Most importantly chakras offer liberation, as we evolve to higher frequencies beyond the worldly. Chakras are a dance of involution and evolution leading to unity consciousness. Unity consciousness is the way forward. I define it as the coming together of the very best wisdom teachings from three sources, ancient tradition, religion and modern day science. I believe we are entering an age of unity consciousness characterised by the universal shift of energy taking us from the war stricken times of the solar plexus to the loving compassionate realm of the heart.

This chapter includes an overview of each chakra, and for a more detailed explanation refer to my previous books *Opening to Spirit* and *Way of the Chakras*. Knowledge of the chakras supports and theoretically underpins E4L. I introduce the characteristics of each chakra and provide a sense of how this ancient system is still relevant and how we can apply this knowledge in our lives today. Starting with the Root chakra all seven main chakras are listed ending with the Crown chakra. The first three chakras are the personal chakras, I think of them as me, myself and I because they relate to survival, self and inner stability. The remaining four are universal chakras.

Root Chakra – Foundation for Life

Sanskrit name	Muladhara
Location	Pelvic floor
Quality	Grounding
Function	Manifestation, taking action
Consciousness level	Egocentric Survival consciousness
Element	Earth
Color	Red
Body Parts	Feet, legs, bones, spine
Balance	Physical health, courageous, practical.
Unbalance	Physical problems, fearful, lethargic

Action is a Root chakra word. Completion and actually getting things done depends on a good flow of energy through your Root chakra. Earth energy is focussed at this chakra and earth energy is about manifestation and bringing things into being. If you think about it we are born from the Root chakras of our mothers. Not only do we come into the world through the Root chakra but everything we wish to create finds completion through Root chakra energy. We often have great ideas which are air energy and we get enthusiastic which is fire energy. As a result we start things that we will never finish unless we can stimulate earth energy and the Root chakra; this is because Root chakra energy is about grounding things in reality. Sometimes we complete things easily. We ground them with little effort. At other times knowing how to work on the Root chakra to help us complete projects can be very useful.

Let's take this book, E4L passed through the idea stage all in my mind, reached the creation stage, I poured energy into it, wrote it and finally arrived at completion. You are reading the book. Energy has flowed freely and E4L has manifested successfully and is being used to enhance lives. This is the process for all things. I think of it as ACT, Always Create Twice, once in your mind and once in the world. Manifestation is all about taking action and creating a powerful foundation for life. This requires downward causation. Energy flows from the universe down to earth. Root chakra energy is important today for its role in completion. If you find yourself not finishing projects, it may be helpful to consider how energy is flowing through your Root chakra. It may be time for you to be really courageous, take a risk and step up in your life. The question to ask yourself here is simply: *what are you going to do and when?*

Sacral Chakra – Sacred Home of I

Sanskrit name	Swadistana
Location	Sacrum/lower abdomen
Quality	Centring
Function	Self-knowledge
Consciousness level	Ego centric – Self consciousness
Element	Water
Color	Orange
Body parts	Womb, bladder, kidneys
Balance	Self love, self knowing, pleasure, express emotions freely, I can attitude.
Unbalance	Low self esteem, constant negativity, emotionless, I can't

You are totally unique, just like everybody else! George Benson sang *"Learning to love yourself is the greatest love of all."*

The Sacral chakra houses the unique self you need to love. This is the centre of self-knowledge. It is about getting to know and love the very essence of who you are. It is about connecting deeply with the spirit that moves through around and as you. Getting to know yourself means taking time with yourself; time for you alone. If you don't want to spend time with yourself, why would anyone else want to? When energy flows freely through the Sacral chakra you will enjoy self-esteem and confidence. You will be able to make your own decisions without fearing what others think. You will value your own opinion and consider outcomes for yourself as well as for others. When you feel at home in the centre of who you truly are, your life will accelerate.

Creativity springs from the well of the Sacral chakra. To create is to bring something new into being. We are all creative in our own unique ways. This can be expressed through the arts, the way we live, the work we do, the children we raise. We can express creativity in many ways, yet so many of us procrastinate. Allowing energy to flow through your Sacral chakra releases your creativity. When you are creative your self-esteem rises. Whenever you say "I can" – the statement of the Sacral chakra – you will feel positive, confident and life will begin improving. Sacral chakra energy is important today because it remains vital to express the creative energy you hold inside.

If you find yourself lacking in Self-love and confidence, focus your attention on your Sacral chakra. A healthy sense of self allows spiritual expansion. When the lower chakras are balanced, energy flows freely through the higher centres, which initiate powerful spiritual growth and success in all areas of your life.

Solar Plexus Chakra– The Power Within

Sanskrit name	Manipura
Location	Base of sternum
Quality	Empowerment
Function	Inner power
Consciousness level	Ego centric – me, myself and I consciousness
Element	Fire
Color	Yellow
Body parts	Digestive organs, eyes
Balance	Express emotion, passion, radiance, conflict
Unbalance	Controlled by emotions, uncaring, depression, violence

The Solar Plexus is found just below your breastbone. It is the radiant sun within your body. When you lift your chest, raise your arms and stretch up in the mornings, you are releasing Solar Plexus energy. The Solar Plexus fuels your body. This natural movement provides a surge of energy that helps you wake up.

Just as the sun provides the earth with power so the Solar Plexus provides your body with power. The Solar Plexus generates energy; it is your body's powerhouse.

The sun gives us light, heat and fuels growth. Without the sun there would be no life on earth. The inner sun is also essential to life; it provides warmth, enthusiasm, passion and inner power. This chakra animates your body and keeps it alive and fired up. The Solar Plexus is the force behind your will. Your will gives you the ability to act consciously, to make decisions and follow them through, knowing you will be successful. This is powerful Solar Plexus energy.

Focus for a moment on a time in your life when you felt powerful. You had a clear vision and followed it; you knew nothing could stop you from achieving your goal. That was your Solar Plexus energy in action.

The Solar Plexus is dominated by fire energy, which gives great clarity and direction, but can also create rage and destruction. Balancing Solar Plexus energy is very important at times of crisis, chaos and instability. Fire energy moves us forward with commitment and assertion. When we connect to the inner power of the Solar Plexus things always get done swiftly. Rapid transformation is a function of this chakra. If you find yourself lacking in commitment and passion, it is time to ignite your inner fire and re-charge your Solar Plexus.

Heart Chakra – True Balance

Sanskrit name	Anahata
Location	Behind physical heart
Quality	Love and compassion
Function	Transformation
Consciousness level	World centric – compassion for all humanity
Element	Air

Color	Green
Body Parts	Heart, lungs, arms, hands
Balance	Unconditional love, balance, truth
Unbalance	Withdrawn, resentful, over analytical

Heart chakra energy is familiar to us all. You already know the heart has many qualities apart from its physical role. We know the feeling of *opening our hearts* or *closing down our hearts.* We know how it feels to have a *broken heart* or how it is to *put our heart fully into something.* Most of us know what it is to *love with all our heart* and the truth expressed when we *cross our heart and hope to die.*

These energetic qualities are stimulated by the Heart chakra. The heart is a great force for change. Moving consciousness to the Heart chakra can help us have a change of heart. We can use air energy to transform the way we think. Thoughts are carried through the air they are powerful forces that have a habit of coming true. When we think *we cannot,* we can't. When you think *you never will,* you won't. When you think *it is too late,* it is too late. When you think you are *not good enough,* you are not good enough. It is for you to change the script, re-write the programme and make the positive changes you need in your thoughts and life. You are the director of your own life. You are the one empowered to make changes. When you know *you can,* you will. When you know *you have all that you need within you,* you can start using it. When you know *you have an abundance of love and compassion,* you can claim it. The Heart chakra is the home of positive change and spiritual transformation.

Here we ascend into the universal chakras. The Heart chakra connects you to the boundless source of love and compassion. It brings balance and elevates consciousness. With Heart chakra energy we reach out with love to embrace all life. At our current stage of human evolution Heart chakra energy is very important.

Many of us have strong Heart chakra energy. Our souls are speeding towards the Divine. We want to move into the heart and love unconditionally. We want to develop ourselves consciously. We have visions of a harmonious planet and are starting to take the necessary steps to create change. We all need love, opening your heart and allowing love to radiate transforms you and changes our world.

Throat Chakra – In the Beginning was the Word

Sanskrit name	Vishudha
Location	Throat
Quality	Vibration
Function	Communication
Consciousness level	World centric–empathy and communion with all life
Color	Blue
Element	Ether
Balance	Harmony, silence, open and expressive
Unbalance	Anxious, restless, find communication difficult.

The Throat chakra is a powerful spiritual centre. Its primary function is communication, initially with the Creator. It also connects you to your inner Self and the *Gift Of Divinity* (GOD) that lies within. This chakra holds answers to many spiritual questions because it allows you to listen as your soul speaks. Through this chakra we can accept our Divine nature. It also facilitates communication with people through words and creativity.

The Throat chakra is responsible for psychic phenomena

connecting people with spirit guides, ancestors, angels and helpers. Psychic communication is far more common than we realise. *Can you remember a time when you thought about someone and they telephoned you, or you sensed something would happen and it did?* We all have a sixth sense that is developed through trusting in its existence. As Dr Wayne Dyer says: *"You will see it when you believe it."*

Ether, the subtlest of the elements, is closely aligned with pure spirit. Ether is a container without it nothing could exist. In science this space is called the quantum vacuum. This container holds information that we can tap into. Have you heard the expression *'It just came out of the blue?'* This saying means information is suddenly remembered or gained seemingly from nowhere. Blue is the Throat chakra colour. Rather than appearing from no-where information literally comes out of the ether. Ether is the original cyberspace, the spiritual superhighway. An archive of everything that was, is and ever shall be, it is known as the Akashic Record or as analyst Carl Jung called it the 'collective unconscious'. A clear flow of energy through your Throat chakra helps you realise your soul purpose and achieve greater all round communication and fulfilment.

In the fast paced world of today many people experience blocks in the Throat chakra. Time and space for spiritual practice is often limited, therefore alienation from spirit results. This causes deep grief and longing. We often reach outside of ourselves trying to fill this gap. It is only when we re-connect with spirit and the soul purpose of life that we feel whole again and grieving ceases. Opening the Throat chakra and resonating fully with the ether element helps us communicate with spirit and elevate consciousness. We communicate with the etheric realm in dreams and meditation.

Brow Chakra – Inner Vision

Sanskrit name	Ajna
Location	Above and between your eyebrows
Quality	Wisdom and knowledge
Function	Inner vision
Consciousness level	Cosmo centric – expanded awareness – heightened spiritual intelligence
Element	Light
Color	Indigo
Body Parts	Left and right cerebral hemispheres
Balance	Insight, knowledge, intuition
Unbalance	Dismissive of your own spiritual experience

What you perceive, you can achieve. The power of the inner eye has been known throughout history. It is the centre of Divine wisdom and knowledge, the home of inner vision. Here you can visualise your destiny and make it reality. This chakra generates lasting peace, which is why advanced meditation practices focus on the inner eye. Meditation can be used as a form of relaxation or taken to another level where it can totally transform your life allowing you to experience and connect deeply with the non-dual aspect of your Divinity. As you open to spirit at this chakra, you will experience an altered state of consciousness and expanded awareness that creates harmony and lasting peace.

The Brow chakra also governs the intellect. When we are able to visualize our direction in life it is easier to walk forward confidently. Positive thinking leads to mastery. You are capable of whatever you put your mind behind. If you believe in failure, failure will hold you in its grip. Likewise success, if you can see it, is yours to embrace. Inner peace and lasting happiness are always available to you. They are your spiritual inheritance.

Without inner vision we stumble in darkness. Not quite knowing why things go wrong in our lives. Not quite knowing which path to take. This chakra balances light and dark, it brings order out of chaos. It helps you face the darkness and find answers to the deeper questions in life. Light can only shine out of darkness. When we are despairing and full of fear, it is time to stop for a moment and re-assess. Meditating on your inner eye shines light into the darkness and illuminates your soul. The answers you have been searching for clearly appear once you begin looking from a place of expanded awareness and spiritual intelligence.

Crown Chakra – Oneness, Peace, Fulfilment

Sanskrit name	Saraswara
Location	Crown of your head
Quality	Fulfilment
Function	Spiritual awareness
Consciousness level	Pure undifferentiated energy, non-dual consciousness
Element	Pure spirit
Color	Violet / gold /white
Body Part	Transcends the physical, relates to subtle anatomy
Balance	Peace, wholeness, liberation, oneness, peak experience
Unbalance	Constant worry, fragmentation, emptiness

The Crown chakra is the seat of pure spirit, the place of fulfilment and spiritual intelligence. When you are ready to connect with your Divine essence and move beyond worldly limitations, you can experience true peace, ecstasy and Divine fulfilment. Attachment to that which changes causes most of the suffering experienced on life's journey. Wealth, status, and material goods can all be taken from us in an instant. It is wise therefore to connect with the power within which transcends ordinary consciousness and brings lasting peace. As humans we long for peace and happiness we want to experience the bliss of wholeness – total absorption in the Divine. However, our attention is often turned away from the Divine placing the happiness we long for out of reach.

By returning to the very core of your being, the chakras, you begin to resonate with a greater power. You can appreciate the movement of all things from pure spirit into gross physical matter (involution) and the return from matter to spirit (Evolution). As our universe takes this journey, we too have a personal voyage. We are born... we live... we die. As long as we live, we are free to move our consciousness through the chakras; to perceive our daily lives from any chakra. Each one has a different lesson and we can become stuck in any chakra. With greater application and awareness, we can learn to balance the flow of energy through the chakras.

Insufficient energy vibrating at the crown maintains imbalances in the chakras below. You will feel bound by limitation and unable to connect with your spiritual energy. Too much Crown chakra energy and it is difficult to live in the world. You become spaced out and ungrounded. As long as you have a physical body, balance between the root and crown chakras is essential to your well-being. Your spirit is a powerful force. When you can ground spiritual energy you can achieve success with ease.

Journey through the Chakras

Journeying through the chakras blesses you at the Root chakra with a strong foundation for life. At the Sacral chakra you come home to the self, developing confidence and self love. This new found energy supports you as you journey to the Solar Plexus where the power within can be expressed. As you continue upwards to the Heart, love and compassion opens as you reach out to the world in Divine service. The Throat chakra is responsible for threefold communication with spirit, self and other people. The beauty is when we can communicate honestly and fully on all three levels. The Brow chakra is the home of expanded consciousness and inner vision. Here we can see the Divine path of life as it unfolds offering us purpose and direction. The evolutionary journey from earth to pure spirit is complete at the Crown chakra offering us a chance to merge and enter non-dual consciousness; the created resting in the arms of the Creator becoming one. This is the teaching.

Personal experience and communication with fellow spiritual travellers suggests it may not be so simple. Resting on the lap of the Creator, blissful experiences, a sense of oneness and non-dual consciousness are seemingly fleeting. I have enjoyed highs, peak experiences, mini Samadhi, glimpses of the Divine. I share a peak experience I had in the next chapter. But all too soon its back to life, back to reality and the world I know and love with all its limitations, irritations and complications. This is life's journey; ascending the chakras living life at each stage, learning the lessons, integrating experiences and then starting all over again. Sometimes we feel as if we have literally gone back to the beginning, but no. We have evolved, we just haven't finished growing. Hence a new look at the ancient chakra system is important.

Unity Consciousness

I think we are moving into an age of Unity Consciousness. I see it as a heightened level of consciousness where we are able to unite the best of Ancient tradition, with the essence of our religions and new findings in science. We are constantly evolving. We are in the 21st Century and live in a very different world to that of our

Ancestors. We have an accumulation of knowledge from throughout the ages that gives us somewhat of a vantage point. We have so much wisdom available to us now. I have the highest respect for the Ancients and the teachings they have left us, much of it has never been surpassed. A lot is still not fully understood, and we continue to shine light on the wisdom traditions of old. There is so much we can draw on. Religions also have a common thread; they provide important moral observances, as well as much needed faith and the ability to connect with a power greater than ourselves. Science also offers interesting research on consciousness studies, the quantum brain, muscle memory and bio-energy. As we evolve it is important to not only transcend our past, but to also include the valuable aspects of that which went before. Unity Consciousness integrates the wisdom of the ages. It synthesizes the richness of our ancient spiritual traditions with the highest call of our religions and the best research from modern science. Unity Consciousness is a powerful way forward.

Theory of Everything

Today's scientists are desperately searching for a Theory of Everything; known as a TOE. They seek to integrate the Newtonian paradigm that says, *'seeing is believing'* and requires evidence of all things, with the quantum world that defies logic suggesting your thoughts are actually creating your reality hence *'believing is seeing'*.

Looking at the chakra system we have the Root chakra, earth energy. It relates to manifestation and the Newtonian material world. It's the slowest and densest energy, the first of seven chakras on our journey of spiritual evolution from earth to spirit. The Crown chakra is first of the chakras on the journey of involution, from spirit to earth. The Crown chakra relates to the quantum realm of subtle energy. The ancient chakra system incorporates so much that it appears to be an original Theory of

Everything.

The chakras are an integral system that supports us on our ever evolving journey of life. We continue to evolve spiritually and continue learning. We are trying to balance our physical Root chakra existence with Crown chakra spiritual transcendence and liberation.

Being and doing in the right quantities remains one of life's mysteries. The theory we know. The challenge is putting it all into practice. Practice is both the challenge and the solution. We can reach peak experience, fully express in the world, even approach self realization, but there appears to be a cycle moving us from the Root chakra to the crown and then back to the root again.

This spiraling journey takes us from embodiment to enlightenment, back to embodiment and then spirals up yet again to the next level. Energy is caused to flow through all the chakras. The ultimate goal of spiritual practice is to transcend this duality by reaching an elevated state of non-dual consciousness, where energy flows in the central neutral column of the chakras called sushumna nadi. This creates One Love, *Atman Jnana* or Self Realization, the highest form of knowledge, knowing that there is no duality. Everything is energy, God, love or however you choose to refer to it.

I am reminded of Buddhist monks who construct intricate, beautifully coloured sand paintings. They spend hours creating finely balanced perfect mandalas and thankas. They meditate on them before sweeping them away. They recognize the impermanence of life. When creating the paintings every effort is made, they give their best and skilfully place every tiny grain of sand achieving perfection. Yet they remain unattached knowing that nothing in the world as we know it lasts forever. It will all be destroyed. Only spirit lives on. Likewise in life the manifest world of the Root chakra is impermanent, but we can still give our best and live a purposeful life. We can enter, like the monks, into the realm of a thousand grains of sand knowing that it will all be swept away one day. Only spirit the universal energy of the Crown chakra non-dual consciousness will remain.

As long as we have a physical body and spiritual aspirations we will be balancing our earthly existence with spiritual potential. Embodiment, the art of appreciating life in your physical body is an essential part of enlightenment, the art of experiencing spiritual elevation and liberation. Continue to journey through the chakras in love and light knowing that you are truly blessed.

Chapter Three

Quantum Divine Mix - Exploring Science and Spirit

"The whole of human philosophy, religion, science, is really nothing but an attempt to get at the right data upon which it will be possible to answer the question and solve, as satisfactorily as our knowledge will allow, the problem of our existence."

Sri Aurobindo

Science and spirituality were once as unlikely partners as chalk and cheese or oil and water. Mentioning both in one sentence was tantamount to sleeping with the enemy for either side. Not anymore. We are witnessing many steps that unite the old with the new and consequently we see the gap closing between science and spirit. New research in quantum physics and advances in neuroscience seem to be saying much of what has already been said in Ancient spiritual teachings.

The Ancients referred to an Akáshic Field and the information it holds. They taught that information on everything that ever was, is, or shall be, is held within the Akashic Record. This field is known in science as the quantum vacuum, a field of energy and in-form-ation. The Ancients spoke of the ability to be in more than one place at the same time. Quantum theory calls this non-locality. The Ancients acknowledged connection and realised that if we hurt another we hurt ourselves because we are all one. This is called entanglement in quantum physics. The Ancients have long held this knowledge sacred and now science is also moving towards this understanding; bridging the gap between science and spirituality.

Quantum Reality

Not only are we seeing more and more people exposed to timeless wisdom via spiritual traditions such as yoga and Buddhism, we are also witnessing quantum physics and developments in neuroscience elucidating some of the Ancient teachings. Quantum physics attempts to discover what the universe is made of, while neuroscience seeks to understand how our brain-mind functions. These are also the primary objectives of contemplative spiritual practices such as Dharana - deep concentration and Dhyana – meditation.

Science seeks information looking outside searching the macrocosm while meditation seeks knowledge from within studying the microcosm. Both methods are based on repeatable empirical evidence not simply on theories and belief systems. Both attempt to measure phenomena that cannot be directly experienced with our five senses. The naked eye cannot see atoms or the energy of science any more than we can see chakras and the energy referred to in spiritual teachings. Both systems use interpretation and reason to better understand our reality. In this way the Ancient spiritual traditions are sometimes seen as the life science technologies of their time.

Einstein's equation $E=mc^2$ means energy can convert to mass and mass can convert to energy. It literally tells us that all matter is energy. Everything you see and touch when broken into subatomic particles is not solid but made from vibrating energy. This energy is the same in you as in the book you are reading and the chair on which you sit. Quantum particles or waves of energy are the fundamental building blocks of all life.

Yoga philosophy also teaches that all life is made of vibrating energy. This energy is known as prana the animating life force. Primal matter (Prakriti) is thought to make up the universe. This matter is made conscious by pure spirit (Purusha), which pervades the universe. Pure spirit is thought to be the true essence or consciousness of humankind. Put simply, all matter including humans are in essence just energy.

Understanding quantum concepts and the philosophy behind yoga and other spiritual traditions can be difficult at first because they require us to make a paradigm shift. We are asked to let go of the outdated Newtonian mechanistic worldview and embrace a new quantum reality. The mechanistic worldview says, if you cannot see that something exists and prove it to be real then it doesn't exist and is not real. In popular language we have the expression: *I'll believe it when I see it.*

Quantum physics shows us something different. Nothing appears to exist, only possibility and potential. We create reality as we know it. The world as we see it is not what it seems. Quantum theory reverses the popular expression, which becomes: *I'll see it when I believe it.* This is because quantum physics reveals that everything is made from energy and that consciousness impacts the energetic field of possibility to create what we think of as reality.

If you have seen the film, *What the Bleep* or *Down the Rabbit Hole,* you will know what I am referring to, as these films illustrate the paradox of what is real and what is not real, really well. I highly recommend them, as audio-visuals can help you understand this new paradigm.

Let's look at the three main concepts of quantum physics to see how the building blocks of the universe behave.

1. **Heisenberg's uncertainty principle** tells us that particles have no definite location; instead they exist everywhere at once. There is no reality, only probability and possibility.

2. **Wave particle duality** particles are affected by and react to observation. Heisenberg said that the path of a moving particle only comes into existence once we observe it. It appears at the subatomic level that reality is created by our

observation.

3. **Non-local correlation** tells us that when particles touch, they become entangled. As a result they can exchange energy and information between them faster than the speed of light and regardless of distance. This transmission of information takes place instantly and beyond the boundaries of time and space. This was considered impossible in the old paradigm.

Can you see how unreal, real really is? It seems nothing is solid there is only energy in its potential state. This energy exists everywhere connecting all things and transmitting information. This same energy changes as we interact with it. This is why in E4L we place so much emphasis on the relationship between our thoughts, beliefs and values. The energy of your thoughts becomes manifest creating the life you live. It seems we programme our destiny with every thought we make, just as this quote by Frank Outlaw expresses:

> *"Watch your thoughts, for they become words.*
> *Watch your words, for they become actions.*
> *Watch your actions, for they become habits.*
> *Watch your habits, for they become character.*
> *Watch your character, for it becomes your destiny."*

From reading this you will have gathered that I am more mystic than scientist. However the point I am making remains, everything is made from energy and reality is created through the impact of consciousness on energy. This is summed up in the following quote.

"Matter as well as mind evolved out of a common cosmic womb...The interaction of our mind and consciousness with the quantum vacuum

links us with other minds around us, as well as with the biosphere of the planet. This openness has been known to mystics and sensitives, prophets and meta-physicians through the ages, but it has been denied by modern scientists... Now, however, the recognition of openness is returning to the natural sciences."

Ervin Lazlo

If spiritual intelligence gained through contemplative practices like meditation helped the Ancients to understand the workings of the universe thousands of years ago. And science is just waking up to this in the last 200 years then surely developing spiritual intelligence will serve us in today's troubled and changing world.

The Meeting of East and West

We are seeing research and dialogue opening between science and spirituality. The emerging dialogue around spirituality asks questions such as, are we genetically coded to be spiritual? Is it an important aspect of human inheritance? Are we hardwired for spirituality? What is consciousness and how can we develop it? What is its relevance to us at this time?

Many are searching for answers to these questions. Harvard educated geneticist Dr Dean Hamer developed the God Gene Theory, in which he suggests spirituality has an innate genetic aspect. According to Hamer certain brain chemicals (monoamines) affect higher consciousness and spirituality. Hamer links the actions of these chemicals to the gene Vmat2, suggesting that spiritual experience is closely linked to our biology. Hamer believes the brain compels us towards spiritual discovery.[1]

Having a high SQ (spiritual intelligence) is thought to give us some evolutionary advantages. Survival rates and greater health benefits are associated with the rituals and behaviours of spirituality.[2] The idea that we are compelled towards higher levels of consciousness and spiritual development is not a new one. It is seen in Abraham Maslow's 'Hierarchy of Needs'.

Psychologist Abraham Maslow is seen as the father of Humanistic Psychology and was apparently an atheist. He is best known for his theory of motivation developed in 1943/54. It is a five step process of evolutionary psychology[3], called the 'Hierarchy of Needs' Using this psychological development model, we can see that our position on it today has certainly evolved since the 1950s, especially in the materially developed world where basic needs are generally met and people are motivated to satisfy their higher needs. See image below.

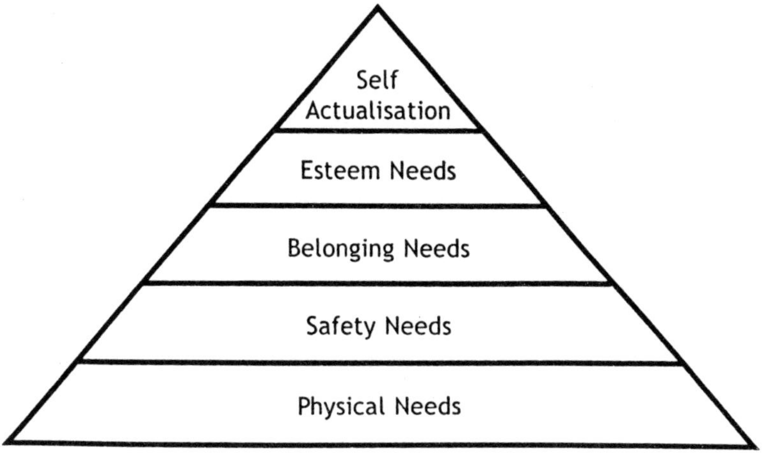

Maslow's Original Hierarchy of Needs

This is Maslow's theory of motivations. At the base of the pyramid are physical and biological needs, food shelter warmth etc. Most of us take this for granted. Therefore we can move up the pyramid to safety needs, this relates to our need for security, order, law and protection, although instability may occur at this level from time to time, mostly protection and safety are givens, freeing us to ascend the pyramid to the need to belong. This is our need to identify with family, friends, and colleagues. It is about the important role of connection, intimacy and relationship. According to Maslow with this need satisfied people progress onto esteem needs. The need to achieve and feel good about oneself, the desire for status and responsibility, this appears to be the home of the ego and success in Maslow's hierarchy. When a level of success has been achieved it is time to move up again, where to this time?

For Maslow the top of the pyramid is the need for self-actualization, which is the pull towards personal growth and fulfilment. To quote Maslow, *"Self Actualization is the intrinsic growth of what is already in the organism, or more accurately, of what the organism is."* (*Psychological Review*, 1949)

I think of self actualization as the need to be all that you can be. It is the need to express your greatest potential and purpose in life. It is the desire to be fully expressed as a human being. The need to self-actualize also causes people to seek spiritual experience. Looking at Maslow's model we certainly appear to have transcended the lower levels and are now in search of something higher.

It is over 50 years since the beginning of the Human Potential Movement and the creation of Maslow's Hierarchy of Needs. Since then people have adapted the model, adding additional stages such as:

- The cognitive need – the desire to know, understand and create meaning.
- Aesthetic need – the search for beauty, balance and form.

And beyond self actualization:

- The need to transcend – which I refer to as spiritual longing.

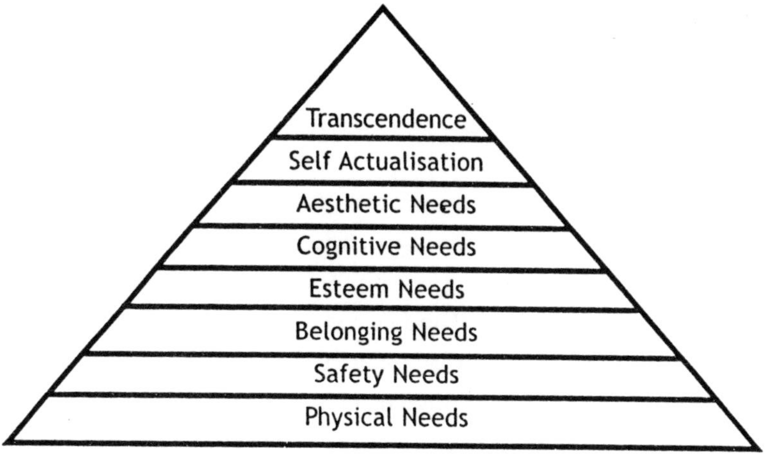

1990s adaptation of Maslow's Hierarchy of Needs

Although these additional stages of motivation have been added it could also be said that cognitive, beauty and transcendence are intrinsic aspects of the need for self actualization.

Maslow's 1950s approach to mapping our development, reminds me of the ancient chakra system which is found in the philosophy and psychology of yoga. The chakra system is an in-depth model for understanding human evolution and spiritual development. The chakra system (which is part of the human energy system) is a seven-stage process of development that culminates, much like Maslow's hierarchy of needs, in self-realization. Self-realization is the aim of many spiritual teachings, elevating consciousness to a place of Satchitanada – existence, knowledge and bliss. This is the consciousness of the Crown chakra or the top of Maslow's evolutionary psychology pyramid. It can also be likened to individuation, which is the culminating stage on Jung's process of human development where an individual reaches a place of self-knowledge and heightened awareness.

These are all states of unity and oneness, where the disparate aspects of self are drawn into a unified whole. This is the aim of all spiritual practice. It is our birthright to know and dwell, at our will, in a state of peaceful bliss. Free to be at one in the realm of non-dual consciousness.

I believe we have all experienced oneness at some point in life. I believe we know peace and bliss intimately and that we search for its return in everything we do, good and bad. Even alcohol and drugs are named spirit and ecstasy. It is this search, this inner knowing that leads us towards spiritual development. Each step we take on life's journey brings us closer to our spiritual essence. At the lowest times in life we seem to connect with an innate faith, we seek the helping hand of our Creator begging to be lifted from our pain. Despair is a lesson that teaches us to move closer to our Creator. The joy and laughter, the pain and tears, all experiences can help us remember our destiny, and realise that we and the Creator are one.

Maslow describes peak experiences as life affirming moments that have their own intrinsic value. From my own experience and discussions with clients, I think of peak experiences as powerful, expansive, open moments, where there is a real sense of connection with all that is. The feeling is positive, pleasurable, a natural high. The moment is suspended in time and space, yet there is a feeling of being so alive and free. There is no fear, no pain, anxiety or doubt. There is a fulfilling presence a beingness that just is. It could be described as orgasmic or drug-free ecstasy, although such descriptions immediately alter the magic. Because the thing about peak experiences is they are a place of knowing beyond description.

Peak experiences provide a heightened, but temporary, level of awareness. Using Eastern terminology we might liken them to a mini Nirvana or Samadhi; a feeling of liberation a glimpse of enlightenment. This is something I think many of us have experienced at some point in our lives. I have enjoyed several peak experiences, when I felt a sense of being totally at one.

In my early twenties I lived with my teacher Swami Joythimayananda and his family in Sri Lanka, where I was studying yoga and naturopathic medicine. It was a troubled time in Sri Lanka with conflict and curfews. So I had the privilege of being the only student staying at the healing centre. I was totally immersed in daily spiritual practice. It was a powerful time of transformation that has continued to serve me throughout my life.

One afternoon while sitting alone on the land in meditation I spontaneously began chanting out loud. Something seemed to sing through me, raising me to another level, filling every cell of my being with vibrant energy. I heard the distant ocean wave through the lush trees. The sun was setting to my right, the sky a deep blue, a faint full moon was beginning to rise and glow to my left. The earth stood strong beneath me and breath breathed me. Then all of a sudden everything merged into one powerful pulsating force, no boundaries existed between me and the earth or the sun, I experienced myself as the moon, the ocean and the sounds. I can't really describe it.... I can only say I was filled with devotion, ecstasy and love and left with an elevated vibration and deep *knowing* that all is one.

Do you remember a time when you felt totally at one with all around you? This happens when the cares of the world are no longer on your shoulders and you have time and space in abundance. It may be during meditation or when you are out in nature. You may be by the sea, on a mountaintop, or in a beautiful forest. The sun may be setting or the full moon shining its bright light. You feel lifted, ecstatic and glad to be alive. Loved and loving all rolled into one. Can you recall such a time? This is an extremely powerful experience. In yoga it is summed up in the mantra 'Soham soham' meaning I am that I am. A peak experience is the place where the experience and experiencer merge. As we evolve spiritually we progress through different levels of awareness and heightened states of consciousness.

We have the ability as humans to elevate consciousness to these heightened states yet we spend most of our time in rather mundane states of ordinary consciousness. Seldom allowing our selves or being willing to honour the heightened magical side of our existence.

Inner Conflict

Entering the magical realm may mean getting out of your head and into your body. The gap between science and spirit is not just external it has an inner reflection. It shows itself in the conflict that can sometimes exist for people between head and heart. The head relates to logic and the rational mind, while the heart is of a more compassionate and loving nature. We are often torn between what the head thinks and the heart feels. What is deemed realistic and what is thought to be unrealistic or too emotional. There is a desire to be in control and get things right. This keeps us in the head and cut off from the body. We may not listen to our inner feelings and gut reactions, favouring logic and reason. Interestingly science is now referring to the heart as a mini brain and the gut as a second brain. The gut is home to neurotransmitters similar to those found in the brain. The body has its own unique intelligence.

We live in a society that rewards logic, not emotions or gut feelings. Children learn early in school that it is right to pride IQ (Intelligence Quotient) over other forms of intelligence such as emotion, intuition, kinaesthetic and the softer spiritual qualities of love and peace. If these other qualities are not also nurtured then their development can become stunted and undervalued. A whole person cultivates all intelligences, including head and heart allowing them to operate harmoniously.

Just as the gap is narrowing between science and spirit we are also seeing biomedical research showing that the gap between head and heart is not as big as previously thought. Research from the Institute of Heartmath in California, states:

- Over 40,000 neurones (brain cells) have been found to exist in the [4]heart, this constitutes a mini brain.
- The heart starts to form in the foetus even before there is a brain
- The heartbeat generates 40-60 times more electrical amplitude than the brain.

As a result of such findings a new branch of medicine known as neurocardiology has evolved.

"The heart is not just a simple pump, but a highly complex, self-organized information processing center with its own functional "brain." With each beat, the heart continuously communicates with the brain and body via the nervous system, hormonal system, bioelectro-magnetic interactions, and other pathways."

Doc Childre, founder of the Institute of Heartmath

Research from HeartMath biomedical center is showing that the heart has its own intelligence and the messages the heart sends to the brain affect physiological regulation and also profoundly influences our perception, emotions, behavior, performance and health.

The Ancients have always understood the importance of the heart. To the Ancient Egyptians the Ab (heart) was the conscience, the self-judging aspect of ourselves that seeks truth. Numerous metaphors have been attached to the heart. The quality of the heart needs little explaining; everyone knows the heart is associated with love, truth and compassion.

Ancient teachings are maintained in popular sayings of today, such as:

- I love you with all my heart
- I give you my heart (love)
- My heart is not in it (lacking motivation)
- Let's get to the heart of the matter (truth)
- Cross my heart (truth)
- Open your heart (compassion)
- My heart was touched (compassion)

These sayings confirm our knowledge of the heart and its wisdom. Touch, the sense associated with the heart, has one of the longest entries in the dictionary. This is due to the breadth of the heart's emotional and energetic qualities. Love and touch contain the potential to open the energy field and allow an increased flow of vital energy. We all need love. We search for it because we feel it has the power to hold everything in balance. Loving touch releases the hormone oxytocin into the body which acts as an antidepressant, raising energy levels and rebalancing the system.

The intelligence of the heart is strong and so powerful that it drives people towards evolving greater connection, meaning and purpose in life. Even when the so-called material successes of life have been achieved if your heart remains heavy there will be no sense of happiness or real fulfilment. Develop a richer experience by honouring your heart and your feelings not just your thoughts.

The Journey of Humanity

Sri Aurobindo in my opening quote speaks of philosophy, religion and science. He mentions their common desire to answer the question of our existence. They each offer something different yet equally valuable. As I look back over the human journey that has brought us this far I see so much that is of great value. I honour the spiritual sciences and philosophies of the Ancients. Teachings from yoga, meditation and healing that when practiced, as the Ancients taught, offer predicable results, just as the sciences of our day.

I am with Sir James Frazer, the social anthropologist and author of *The Golden Bough* (1922) who asks, *"if under science we may include those simple truths, drawn from observation of nature, of which men in all ages have possessed a store."*

Sir James Frazer noted that as humans we have traveled through three ages. I honour them all. It is my understanding that when we can embrace the very best of human history, combining something from each of these ages:

1. **Age of Magic** – holistic teachings from our Ancient spiritual traditions
2. **Age of Religion** – ethical codes and essence of our major religions
3. **Age of Science** – advances of modern science and technology

Then we will emerge as the fully conscious beings we have the potential to be. When the power from all three ages is integrated and science and spirituality merge we will create an important synergy and make a huge shift in our consciousness. It is this transformation, this quantum divine mix, which I refer to as Unity Consciousness. And to reach it we must honor our history and embrace spiritual knowledge in this age of science. This was alluded to by one of the greatest scientists of our era, Einstein:

"I never came upon any of my discoveries through the process of rational thinking."

Einstein

Chapter Four

Energy and Ecstasy - the Power of Sacred Union

"According to the Tao and even according to modern physics the world is continually pulsating, when we orgasm, we harmonise not only with our partner but with the world and its pulsations."
Mantak Chia

Sexuality and the ability to reproduce ourselves have been revered throughout history. Sexual energy, the primal power responsible for your very creation, is one of the most powerful energies we have. Without it you would not exist, you stand as a testament to its power. Sexual energy not only weaves you into being, it continues to serve your body, mind and spirit, producing health, happiness and fulfilment. This potent force impacts all the chakras flowing from the root to the crown and then returning from crown to root.

Sexual energy holds numerous benefits and pleasures, bestowing excitement, balance, healing and the potential for bliss and spiritual ecstasy. Yet like fire, passion and losing control, sexual energy is often feared, suppressed, exploited and abused. One of our most beautiful, creative and loving attributes can be left dormant, misunderstood and mistreated. Or as Osho said, used merely as a sleeping pill!

I was taught by my yoga teacher Swami Vishnudevananda, who advocated celibacy, that orgasm is the closest many people ever come to Nirvana or Samadhi; these are the highest states in Buddhist and Vedantic teachings respectively. He likened this place of complete surrender and letting go into nothingness and simply becoming one with all that is, to orgasm. I had difficulty understanding why some yogic teachings and religions promote sexual abstinence, while others revere this creative force.[1] They all seem aware of its capacity to bring about spiritual ecstasy and blissful states.

Primal Instincts

Most of us will take every opportunity we get to glimpse the adult body in all its naked beauty. It stimulates our primal instincts and arouses a sense of pleasure. As sexual energy streams through our bodies we come alive, of course it's because of sexual chemistry and sacred union that we *are* alive. Sex is part of our very essence, we are sexual beings.

Sexual energy has remained a primal and powerful force for thousands of years. From the very beginning of time in one form or another sex has enjoyed a high profile. Sexually explicit images are seen as bas-reliefs on ancient temple walls, the visual media of the Ancients. The phallus and the yoni were revered throughout the ages. The Ancient Egyptians erected obelisks and early matriarchal societies sculpted female genitalia. Festivals still exist in Africa and Asia where larger than life sacred genitals are carried through the streets as symbols of fertility and prosperity. Today the near naked body is seen on billboards everywhere, selling dreams, youth and consumer goods little has changed.

The recognition of our sexual power and passion is ever present, but how this energy is used or abused has taken on a new form. We live in times and societies where what was once sacred is now often undermined and exploited. Ecstasy has become a drug, instead of an exalted frequency of energy. To enter ecstasy is to be ex-static – without stasis ie. vibrating at a heightened level of consciousness.

Sexual language and images were originally used to portray not only our physical beauty, but also our spiritual essence. Sex was acknowledged as a tool to express love and reach exalted states of consciousness. The Kulachakra Tantra states: "*The lotus flower is an ocean filled with bliss, when it is united with the sceptre, pure knowledge arises which explains the nature of all things.*" Now we hear "*I want to sex you up*" or "*I am your sex-o-matic Venus freak*". Such lyrics suggest an unenlightened attitude towards sexuality. They tell us that our appetite for sensuality and sexuality has not waned but our awareness of sex as a sacred ritual has definitely decreased.

When we look back at our spiritual traditions we find a rich archive of sacred sexuality. Tantric yoga offers spiritual teachings from West Africa, Ancient Egypt and India. We are taught to honour our bodies as sacred temples and learn to elevate the energy that flows through the Chakras. In so doing we will reach our highest potential as Divine human beings. The Ancients recognized sexual energy as the most powerful spiritual tool we have and they used it with wisdom. In this Yoruba[2] myth Osun as the temptress uses female sexuality for the good of civilization.

Ogun, the fiery Orisha entered the forest following a fight with Shango who was having an affair with Ogun's ex wife. Due to Ogun's role in preparing the path for civilization, all the Orishas missed him. When he refused to return, they decided to go and fetch him. Orunmila, an elder and master of divination went first and failed. Ogun remained after several Orishas' attempts. As civilization halted, the beautiful goddess Osun asked her elders for permission to go and get Ogun. Permission was granted.

Osun tied five silk scarves around her waist, and placed a pot of honey beneath them. She ran singing and dancing into the forest. Ogun heard her songs and smelled the sweetness of honey. He became intoxicated with desire. Osun danced and Ogun followed. As he approached she wet his lips with honey. Osun tied the scarves together and led Ogun back to civilization. Ogun followed his senses. As he left the forest and greeted the Orisha, he saw much to his dismay that Osun having achieved her goal had disappeared. [3]

The same power used by Osun is seen in our media today. Women sit on cars and men come out of the forest to buy them. But in this myth, we see Osun's power directly contributing to the evolution of civilization. We also see her maintain the balance of male and female energy. Osun, doesn't say, "forget it, I'll do his work myself". Instead Ogun is returned to his role. We can all embrace our sexuality, power, beauty and the spirit that moves through us. We can also acknowledge as the Ancients before us the potency of sexual energy and its ability to elevate body, mind and spirit. We can raise our sexual energy and ecstasy to the heights of spiritual fulfilment.

Body/Health – Personal Chakras

When sexual energy is allowed to flow freely through the Root, Sacral and Solar Plexus chakras, health and wellbeing is generated. These three chakras are personal energy centers relating to physical health, sexual and reproductive health, plus passion and confidence. On a physical level, sexual energy, also known as Ching Chi or Eros, has numerous benefits. It's a healing energy offering to uplift, re-vitalise and totally re-energize your system. And if that's not enough research also suggests that sexually active people live longer, happier and healthier lives.

When sexual energy is expressed through lovemaking the parasympathetic nervous system (PSNS) our internal brake, is activated. The PSNS has a relaxing and cleansing effect on the body: it reduces anxiety and gives way to a sense of calm. It's the perfect tool for stress management. Sexual arousal requires a level of relaxation; a shift that invites energy to flow from the head down to the genitals. The genitals have the capacity, unlike the head, to amplify and concentrate energy. We often have too much energy in the head, worrying, stressing and trying to work out our next move. This dispersal of energy offers a welcome balance. Lovemaking reduces stress and tension in the body;

while orgasm redistributes blocked energy, creating release and re-establishing flow. That's why the Ancients developed sexual practices. They saw them as a means for cultivating self, transforming energy and reaching higher states of consciousness. From the gentle touch of a lover's hand, the soft gaze of an eye, to passionate lovemaking, sexual energy plays a role in our lives like no other.

Loving Touch

Touch, our first sense to develop in the womb, is recognised for its ability to bring comfort. Sharing loving touch nourishes the entire being. Touching releases the hormone oxytocin, sometimes known as the hormone of love or the cuddle hormone. It plays a part in maternal instincts, sexual arousal and bonding.

Over the last ten years neuroscientists have found oxytocin receptors in the brains and reproductive systems of both males and females.[4] Oxytocin may be responsible for the feeling of connection we have after making love. The more a couple make love, the deeper the bond. This connection can cause just seeing each other to release oxytocin, heightening the desire to be together even more. Maybe this explains what we call falling in love? Couples who literally stay in touch, create lasting harmonious relationships. Holding hands, cuddling, stroking, kissing, massage and generally nurturing with loving touch increases production of the love hormone and strengthens intimate bonds. We all know couples who have been together forever and remain affectionate and happy in each other's company. It seems touch is the secret.

As well as being good if a lasting relationship is your desire, the love hormone is also credited with inducing calm, reducing stress, acting as a natural antidepressant and lowering cravings and addictions. Touch is truly uplifting, bringing an abundance of pleasure and wellbeing.

Eye Contact

Sexual energy is often expressed through fire in the eyes, a lingering glance, a flirtatious stare or the loving embrace of meeting eyes. It is said the eyes are the windows to the soul, when eyes connect intimately so much love can be communicated. Eye contact speaks deeply to the soul and is an important aspect of how couples relate. Holding eye contact with the one you love opens your heart and has a powerful healing effect on the body.

We each have a desire to be seen, recognized and loved. We want to be held in our vulnerable beauty. The eyes have a unique language a fiery and passionate mode of communication they invite, caress and adore, they glow, sparkle, witness and approve. The eyes speak while bodies listen. Giving or receiving a charged glance communicates so much. The eyes have a truth all of their own. When we can see and be seen, body awareness and sense of self improves, esteem rises. Confident eye contact between lovers is a great way of expressing and raising sexual energy.

Health Benefits of Orgasms

Health is enhanced by touch, awareness raised by being seen and the intense expereince we call orgasm has the potential to not only raise vitality levels but connect us to the world and rhythm of the universe. According to Taoist Master and sexual health expert Mantak Chia: *"Multiple orgasms are part of the unfolding process of becoming one with each other and the world."*

Orgasm is the climatic peak and spontaneous letting go of the body/mind into joyous euphoria. It is known as the fountain of youth and thought to be essential for the health and wellbeing of both men and women. The rhythmic contractions of orgasm bring a release of energy shifting brain waves into an altered state of consciousness. Chemicals are released in a burst of energy followed by spontaneous deep relaxation. Orgasm invites you to let go into a vast, unbridled, oceanic experience that can be profoundly healing.

During orgasm the whole system is flooded with ecstatic energy. All the energy pathways and cells in the body open to receive the Divine elixir and are realigned at the point of ecstasy. Pioneer of western body-centred psychotherapy, William Reich, found in his research on bioenergy, that sex and particularly orgasms were crucial for the bioelectric current of energy to complete its circuit through the body.[1] He saw this flow of energy as essential for health.

Ancient traditions have complex energy maps detailing pathways which energy flows through. I have learned from my work with energy that it is not so much the differing maps, meridians, nadis, etc., but the contraction and expansion of energy, found in all traditions, that holds vital importance. Sexual Energy in the teachings of the Ancient Egyptians, the Taoists and Tantric yogis of India is seen to flow in a rhythmic pattern of expansion and contraction.

In nature, day expands until it contracts into night, the moon expands in fullness and then again contracts into darkness. Flowers rise and blossom then wilt and return to the earth. In your body blood flows out from your heart and returns via your veins, your lungs expand and contract keeping you alive. All nature expands out until it reaches a point of resistance and then contracts again to the core. We all expend energy for approximately twelve hours and then contract energy in sleep renewing our resources for another day. Day becomes night and night day. This is the underlying rhythm of all life and the cosmos, a constant flow of expansion and contraction. This rhythm is expressed through sexual energy and orgasm has the role of amplifying this wavelike rising and falling motion.

Mind/Happiness – Interpersonal Chakras

The interpersonal chakras are the Solar Plexus, Heart and Throat.

As sexual energy flows freely through them we experience feelings of happiness, love and opening into expansive energy. Sexuality is not limited to the physical it extends to the psyche. The mind plays a major role in how sexual energy is expressed and experienced. The more comfortable you are with your sexuality the more positive psychological benefits flood your system. Feel-good chemicals are released raising self esteem, confidence and generating happiness.

Awakening sexual energy can be very liberating and uplifting. Sharing love intimately in a loving relationship can create ecstasy and transformation. While the physical body generates sexual energy the mind transforms it. Your capacity to create ecstasy and transform sexual energy will depend on your childhood experience of touch, love and affection.

The Sacral chakra starts to awaken activating sensuality and sexual energy in the years between seven and fourteen. The sensual desire for safe touch, hugs and affection begins in these early years. This is not sexual energy in an adult sense, but the beginning of what will become sexual expression. It's so important that young people witness and experience healthy interpersonal relationships. Appropriate touch, hugs and affection need to be freely shared in a loving and safe way.

What was your early experience of touch, love and affection? Take a moment to ask yourself this question. Think about the years between seven and fourteen, was this a happy time in your life? What impressions did you receive? Was energy allowed to flow in a loving manner or was loving sensual energy held back and restricted? Did you see your parents embrace and openly show affection? What morals persisted in relation to sexuality? Was your experience of sexuality distorted in an abusive manner removing innocence and creating confusion? Did you feel accepted and loved as you developed into a man or a woman?

Our early patterns of behavior and experiences have a profound impact on us shaping our adult expectations. In order to open into a more fully expansive experience of sexuality it may be necessary to release outdated beliefs. You may be holding onto values, beliefs and scripts that no longer serve you. I offer more detail in the chapter on Energy Psychology.

The beauty of E4L is that we work from a purely energetic perspective, recognizing that everything is energy, even outdated beliefs that appear to be holding us back are just energy, and the nature of energy is that it can change in an instant, in fact that's all it's ever doing. So prepare to release and let go, there's no need to re-tell and re-live experiences or get caught up in the story. You just need to transform the energy. Practice the Energy Release Technique in chapter seven. This is a powerful, quick acting tool you can use that allows you to shift energy and release anything that no longer serves you.

Releasing negative energy creates space for greater happiness. Sexual energy amplifies emotion. Whatever you feel, whether its pleasure or pain, love or anger it will be magnified. So it's vital to release energy you don't need, purifying your system and preparing to embrace and amplify positive vibrations.

The feeling of love is amplified during lovemaking, happiness is amplified, as is sadness and grief, all feelings expand. That is why intimacy can create feelings of real vulnerability. Old fears emerge. Typically men have fears around performance and women around attractiveness; even though performance and attraction are direct results of our levels of sexual energy rather than anything to do with our partners. The challenge is to accept ourselves as totally unique and beautiful. Know that no one else can give and receive as you do. No one expresses themselves like you. No one looks like you, because there is only one YOU. Allow sexual energy to flow freely through your interpersonal chakras, enhancing sexual expression, expanding your love for self, your partner and the universe we all share. Let sex be a healing elixir that raises energy levels and increases happiness, a medicine for your body, mind and spirit.

Spirit/Fulfilment – Transpersonal Chakras

Sexual energy and the Divine life force are known to be one and the same. Sexual union goes beyond the physical to become a Divine ritual. In line with the laws of nature, sex draws energy from the centre of your being out into the universal force field. Energy is replenished and returns to the core, bringing healing and heightened awareness of the transpersonal chakras.

Your transpersonal chakras are the Throat, Brow and Crown. As sexual energy flows freely through them you have the potential to reach infinite heights. Expanding energy through the conscious act of making love propels you into a vast ocean of perfect connection, bliss and oneness. For a moment the created is one with the Creator, at home in the arms of the Divine.

In Ancient traditions the lover was worshiped as the Divine. Your partner was seen as an embodiment of the Divine male or female, a God or Goddess. Divine couples such as Shiva and Shakti in India and Ausar and Auset in Egypt, (also called Isis/Osiris) are seen to reach heightened states of consciousness in union. Sexual union is a sacred act, providing a beautiful way of connecting with and raising soul consciousness.

The oldest spiritual belief, found in cultures all around the world, is the coming together of male and female energies to create life. The masculine pure undifferentiated energy known as Purusha is charged with the feminine life-giving force of Prakriti. The male represents stillness and potential waiting to be aroused by the active feminine. This is the initial Divine polarity that brings everything we know into being. It is the yin and yang from which all else arises.

Purusha corresponds to infinite spirit existing beyond, space, time and creation. The uncertain potential and possibility mentioned in quantum physics. Prakriti corresponds to matter, that which is bound by space, time and creation, that which we think of as real.

Think of the Crown chakra and its infinite potential and the

Root chakra as the physical manifestation of spirit. As we acknowledge this polarity, Sri Aurobindo also advises: "*Both spirit and matter exist and are indissolubly welded, precisely because they are simply one thing viewed from two sides. The distinction between them is one of the primary dualisms and a first result of the great ignorance.*" Conscious lovemaking re-enacts the primordial unity, joining male and female in an ecstatic embrace. Honouring and adoring your lover as the Divine and reaching heights of ecstasy together are ways to embody spirit. When viewed as sacred sex can become union and communion with the Divine. Like daily bread, it will feed your body mind and spirit. In Taoist teachings sexual union is a morning prayer because of its ability to uplift and energise the spirit preparing your system for a perfect day. Sexual union with your life partner generates a powerful exchange of loving energy that has the potential to be exalted connecting us with a pure universal love and ecstasy that can radiate to all beings.

Three Types of Orgasm

At the spiritual level orgasm is no longer limited to the physical. Orgasm is said to be without limits, embracing the beginning and end of the universe and then returning again and again. This is true for both men and women although multiple orgasms are more common in women.

There are three main types of orgasm: physical, psycho-emotional and spiritual. They expand sequentially each one transcending and including the others. Physical orgasm is the first and most familiar. It can be experienced in the genitals as spontaneous sensations and elevated levels of pleasure. The second is the psycho-emotional, energy moves up to the heart and orgasm is accompanied by a sense of expansion and overwhelming feelings of love, compassion and ecstasy. When energy radiates out from the heart, orgasm can be experienced by the entire body, the peripheries of the body fingers, toes and everything in between tingle and vibrate in a harmonious rhythm connecting you more deeply at the heart level with your partner. The third is spiritual, energy continues to rise through the chakras allowing a fountain of orgasmic energy to be experienced from the brow and crown chakras. In this state, total merging and union with your partner is experienced. There is no longer a sense of you and another but total absorption and oneness. As energy flows at this level of consciousness there is union with pure undifferentiated spirit, a blissful resting in the Divine, a peak experience.

Evolution of Sexual Ecstasy

The Hevajra Tantra states: "*that by which the world is bound, by that same its bonds are released*". The quote refers to the senses and the ability for us to become liberated by them. Becoming aware of sexual energy and truly honouring the sacred within each moment of conscious, nurturing, love making increases health and extends the quality and length of life as well as bringing pleasure, happiness and fulfilment.

The tantric masters advocated a four-fold evolution of ecstasy. The journey begins in the physical, awakening the senses with an erotic smile. Secondly the emotions are aroused with a longing gaze, followed thirdly by burning passion and the intimate embrace. Eventually the physical is transcended as fourthly, the loving couple enter sacred union, rising into bliss and fulfilment.

Higher transcendent places are reached as a result of cultivating the three levels of sexual energy – physical, psycho-emotional and spiritual.

1. **Embodiment** learning to embrace pleasure, love and ecstasy by being fully present and conscious. Energy and ecstasy requires embodiment, enhanced awareness and comfort in your physical body.

2. **Intimacy** the ability to open emotionally to sharing love with your partner and really allowing yourself to see and be seen.

3. **Spiritual expansion,** conscious loving invites you to open to spirit reaching elevated levels of consciousness.

Conscious lovemaking is active meditation. Use the exercises below to raise energy and cultivate ecstasy.

Exercises for Enhancing Energy and Ecstasy

Cultivate Self Love with the Inner Smile

This active meditation aids embodiment and cultivates Self love. It takes you on a journey through your chakras connecting with your organs which store emotional energy. Tension and negative energy transform as you are bathed in restoring and loving inner smiles. Your organs are lovingly thanked for all they do. Familiarize yourself with the location of your major organs before you begin.

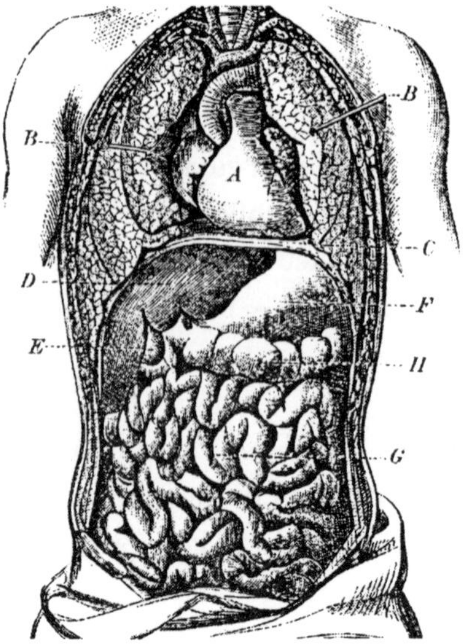

Major Internal Organs

A. Heart
B. Lungs drawn aside
C. Diaphragm
D. Liver
E. Gall bladder
F. Stomach
G. Small intestines
H. Large intestine

Prepare for this practice by sitting in a meditative posture or lying down relaxing your entire body. Make sure your arms and legs are relaxed, not crossed. Your pelvis and chest are relaxed. Release any tightness around your abdomen, lengthen your spine, neck and allow your face to be soft and relaxed. Take a nice deep breath. Inhaling through your nose, abdomen up, exhaling through your nose abdomen down. Relaxxxx.

Starting with your Root chakra, bring awareness to your pelvic bowl, your genitals, glands-ovaries or testes. Let your smiling energy expand creating a loving glow. Visualize the red ray. Give thanks as you allow the energy to anchor your legs and feet.
Raise your energy and smile into the Sacral chakra. Smile into your lower abdomen, large intestine, womb, kidneys, adrenal glands and bladder. Visualize the orange ray, giving thanks and allowing energy to flow freely deep within.

Smile into your Solar Plexus. Smile and thank your hard working digestive organs, your stomach, liver, gall bladder, pancreatic gland and intestines. Visualize the yellow ray lighting up your abdominal cavity as energy radiates out.

Draw energy up to your Heart chakra. Smile and thank your life-giving heart and lungs, your spleen, thymus gland and trachea. Visualize the green ray, feel your organs expand and contract as energy fuels your entire body.

Feel energy rise to your Throat chakra. Smile into your pharynx, larynx, epiglottis, thyroid and parathyroid glands. Visualize the sky blue ray and the smiling energy as it soars through your throat. Give thanks, release and say "*Aaahh*".

Lift energy now to your Brow chakra, your inner eye. Smile and thank your brain, hind, mid and frontal. Thank your pineal gland, neurones and nerve pathways. Visualize the indigo ray the darkness from which light emanates and floods your whole being.

Finally the Crown chakra. Smile into your thousand petaled lotus. Let the top of your head and pituitary gland smile. Visualize the cascading ray of liquid gold as it erupts from your crown and pours over your body in a smiling embrace.
Smiles are in abundance and like healing elixir they communicate loving kindness to every cell in your body. As this powerful energy radiates out your smile delivers a message of unconditional love and acceptance of self and all beings.

Lovers Gaze to Cultivate Intimacy ...'in-to-me-see'

The more we can love and accept ourselves as wonder-filled, beauty-full, vulnerable and passionate beings the more we can accept others as exactly that. We are each the very essence of the Divine, Gods and Goddesses longing to be loved. We long to be seen and accepted for who we truly are in our wholeness. This exercise invites you and your lover to hold each other in a passionate lovers' gaze.

Take a moment to get comfortable together, lie down or sit opposite each other crossed-legged with your hands gently touching. This is a time and space for the two of you to just be. There is no pressure to speak, caress or do anything just bask in the loving gaze of your Divine life partner.

As your eyes meet, hold your gaze, relax, be open to all sensations, look deeply, allowing yourself to fully see and be seen. Welcome the intimacy as your eyes connect and your hearts open. This is a meditation like no other softly embracing your lover in your gaze. The lover merging with the beloved, enjoy the energetically charged silence as time stands still. Allow energy to reveal your deep connection, as one.

This is a strong bonding exercise. It reminds your brain and body of those first months of life, when psychologists believe we don't know we are separate from our mother. Gazing into your lover's eyes with tenderness and warmth creates oneness and connects you intimately.

Lovers Touch – Embracing Love and Ecstasy

A lover's touch satisfies many needs, it offers comfort and sanctuary, love and kindness, excitement and pleasure. When fused with the sacred it can raise your level of consciousness to a place of total bliss. This exercise asks you to explore loving touch with your life partner in an embrace of love and ecstasy.

Again this is an active meditation, offered as a prayer to your Divine lover. It allows you to enter into a space of living, loving and learning together. Prepare sacred space in a way that pleases you both, using candlelight, incense and music. Make sure the room is warm and that you will not be interrupted by children or other curious individuals.

This exercise has seven stages which each need to be honoured. Bathe and oil your bodies before you begin. Prepare to touch yourself and your life partner in a deeply loving way. Take this opportunity to explore, use your hands as messengers for your senses. Let your hands see the beauty, hear the music, taste the sweetness and smell the aroma of the sacred body temple beneath them. Learn to dance in a rhythm of ecstasy. Touch from the top of the head to the tips of the toes, exploring each and every part. Use your hands to stroke gently, awaken, navigate, penetrate, stimulate, love, brush, sculpt, trace, feed and nourish your soul.

1. Both of you take time to look before you touch, feasting your eyes on your partners sacred body temple

2. Touch yourself from head to toe, as your partner learns what pleases you
3. Allow your partner to touch you from head to toe, following your lead
4. Watch your partner as they touch themselves, from head to toe. Learn what pleases
5. Lovingly touch your partner utilising lessons learnt
6. Share loving touch together now in a harmonious buffet of love
7. Continue with lovemaking

Loving touch is an important part of conscious relationship. It raises body awareness and confidence levels as well as communicating trust and love. Touch builds and maintains health, wellbeing and fulfilment.

We are specifically hardwired to experience love and ecstasy. Science[5] has found specific, (non-myelinated therefore slow conducting) nerves in the skin known as C Tactile fibres. These nerve fibres are totally separate from the myelinated sensory nerves in the skin and they respond directly in the brain, triggering emotions of pleasure, romantic love and sexual arousal. This exercise helps keep the fires burning for lasting love and ecstasy.

Remember all these exercises are active meditations, powerful tools for opening to the energetic spirit that flows through, around and as you. These are practices for lovingly honouring your Divine life partner and raising consciousness.

Energy and Ecstasy asks us to acknowledge our powerful sexual energy. It invites us to build awareness of its many physical benefits and embrace the pleasure and happiness it brings. Most of all, this chapter calls for us to reinstate the sacred role of sexual energy in our lives. As we ride the energetic wave of orgasm into ecstasy we have the potential to be at one with all that was, is and ever shall be.

Living Consciously in the 21st Century

"To lose one's health renders science null,
art inglorious, strength unavailing,
wealth useless and eloquence powerless."
***Herophilius** (Greek Physician)*

Energy crisis is not limited to melting ice caps and carbon footprints; it shows up much closer to home. Low energy levels threaten to destroy health, relationships and in some cases sanity. With personal energy resources on the decline and people frequently complaining about not having enough energy or time to fully enjoy life, something has to change. Do you ever find yourself feeling overworked, overwhelmed and generally a bit on the grumpy side? Maybe, just a bit! Then perhaps it's time to commit to raising your energy and living consciously in the 21st Century.

We are vibrational beings and our health is reliant on high frequency, free flowing energy moving through the body, mind, spirit continuum. So why do some people live high-energy lives while others are forever tired and lacking in energy? From researching life energy and working with people to improve their health and wellbeing, I have identified four major ways people prevent energy from flowing.

1. **Physical blocks** – holding stress and tension in the body
2. **Psycho-emotional issues** – holding onto negative thought patterns
3. **Diet** – poor eating habits what, how, where and when you eat
4. **Lack of rest** – constantly doing things! Always being prepared for action.

It's simple really, when our frequency of energy is low and the flow is restricted in any way our health starts to diminish Therefore increasing the vibration and maintaining energy flow supports health and wellbeing.

To quote Dr Valerie Hunt, *"The healthy body is a flowing, interactive electrodynamic energy field. Motion is more natural to life than non-motion; things that keep flowing are inherently good. What interferes with flow will have detrimental effects."*

Why wait to get ill before taking care of your life? E4L Conscious Living Programme advocates energy education for all the family, providing simple energy techniques to restore flow, enhance health and help you avoid stress and illness forever.

It makes sense that health, happiness and success are achieved when vibrations are high and energy is flowing at an optimum level. To achieve this we use our four main modalities. Each combating one of the four ways people restrict energy flow. The modalities are listed below and detailed in the following four chapters.

Energy 4 Life Modalities

Energy Exercises
Energy Psychology
Energy Foods
Energy Balance

The modalities form the E4L Natural Healthcare System and can be used for:

Healing and Restoration returning the body to optimum health.
Maintenance and Prevention to ensure that the body stays healthy
Enhanced Health wellbeing of body, mind and spirit

Any disturbance to the even flow of energy can lead to dis-ease. The Ancients told us that all illness is caused by a disturbance in the flow of energy. Living life to the full requires you to be conscious of the flow of energy throughout your body, mind and spirit. This is the secret to good health. It's all about creating ease within, because when you are not creating ease in your life you are creating dis-ease. This is why we say health is wealth. No amount of money can buy health, time or energy. It is senseless to lose your health, time and energy in the pursuit of wealth.

The four modalities impact all areas of life. Focusing on energy directs us to the very heart of our existence and provides a simple alternative to how we view and cope with life. How are you using your energy and how could you use it better, is the question? E4L offers a paradigm shift a new and conscious way of looking at life's many ups and downs.

The solutions E4L offers stand the test of time. They are embraced from the East and West as well as from Ancient and contemporary practices that can help you transform energy, re-fuel, find inner stability and create balance in this fast changing world. High-energy people, exude vitality, passion and enthusiasm, all ingredients required for success. E4L is the practical conscious remedy for personal energy crisis. So let's explore the first of four E4L modalities.

Chapter Five

Energy Exercises – Honouring your Physical Temple

Health is Wealth
People lose their health trying to get wealthy
and then spend their wealth reclaiming their health!
Anon

Your Sacred Body Temple

Your physical body is a sacred temple to be loved and honoured. It is the first gift you receive from life. Imagine being consumed by pain as a result of losing your health, nothing else would matter. So it is vital to restore and maintain the health of your physical vehicle. After all, you cannot have a spiritual experience without it.

Learning to love and honour your body requires you to be present in it, at home in your own skin. We all have something about our bodies we don't like. But when it really comes down to it our bodies serve us well and that's what matters.

Bodies do an amazing job of taking us where we want to go. They constantly prevent bacteria from invading. They digest food, even when it's barely recognizable as food. They eliminate waste and toxins, keep us breathing, and they process our emotions so that we can feel good. Our bodies balance a whole cocktail of hormones and neurotransmitters so that you never really get too hot or cold, too wet or dry, they let us reproduce, and that's only some of the things we need to thank our bodies for. Oh and your hands, muscles, eyes and complex brain are allowing you to read this page. And we complain about our appearance. Your body is awesome! It is to be loved, honored and revered. Take a moment now to breathe deeply and give thanks. Wow! What a great gift it is to have a physical body and be alive in this moment.

When you feel good about your body by raising your body awareness the odd few pounds seem so insignificant. Don't get me wrong if you really have things you need to change about your body for health reasons then go ahead. But if it's just the usual "I want to look like celebrity X" then get over it and give thanks for the unique sacred temple you have been blessed with.

Each day your amazing body temple is changing, that is its nature. It grows, it maintains and it dies. Yes, even as you read, parts of you are changing and parts are dying. Yoga texts tell us that for the first 18 years of life we are growing, constantly creating new cells. From the years 18 to 35 we are maintaining, which means as cells die they are renewed. From 35 onwards we are decaying. That means more cells are dying than being renewed. Energy Exercises help preserve the body by prolonging the maintenance stage. Isn't that a blessing!

What are Energy Exercises?

Energy Exercises are an eclectic blend of gently flowing movements and stretches. Each is designed to release tension and enhance energy flow. Energy Exercises are generally yin in nature because they draw energy in and calm the system. They can also be dynamic and designed to stimulate and release energy.

The exercises are drawn from culturally diverse, Ancient and contemporary systems of healthcare. Many are from yoga and chi gong others I have personally developed. The concept of Energy Exercise has stood the test of time. They are alive today because they are simple to learn, safe to practice and highly effective.

The exercises relate to the five elements, earth, water, fire, air and ether or the scientific version, solid, liquid, heat, gas and space. The body is made of these five elements, each relating to one of the Chakras[1]. In all aspects of E4L we work directly with the flow of energy, we don't use complex names and complicated energy maps. We simply aim to encourage the contraction and expansion of energy through the body, mind, spirit continuum. This rhythm is the underlying factor shared by all energy systems. The maps are different in various systems like Ayurveda, Acupuncture and Polarity Therapy yet they are all effective. This confirms that the map is not the territory. Hence in E4L we work directly with the universal rhythm found in all life forms – expansion and contraction.

Energy Exercises and the Breath

One of the best ways to tap into energy is through the breath. The breath creates an interface between your body and mind. When Energy Exercises stretch the body they also positively affect the mind. Your conscious mind and your unconscious mind are also linked by the breath. Breathing is the only autonomic function of the body that we consciously control. (Apart from the anal sphincter muscle and look how hard that was to control!) You cannot for example control your liver or your intestines, they are autonomic. So when you consciously control your breath, you are automatically tapping into your nervous system and bringing it under your control as well. That is why the breath is used so much to change moods, calm panic-attacks or enter a meditative state.

And of course the breath is closely connected with energy and spirit. The Sanskrit word Prana, Chinese – Chi, Egyptian - Shekem, Yoruba – Asé are all words that mean energy – the life-force. Even in English we have the word respiration, coming from the latin spiritus meaning spirit, life-force.

When we are born it is the breath successfully entering the body that signals life and at the end of life's journey we take our last breath. There is a crucial relationship between energy, breathing and life itself. Therefore in E4L and Energy Exercise in particular, attention to breathing is vital.

Self-Regulation

Energy Exercises stimulate the crystal like (piezoelectric) properties of the body. The body's connective tissues form a crystalline matrix that communicates with all cells. It is known that piezoelectric crystals generate electric fields when they are stretched and compressed. These fields carry information to all the body's cells.

"It is as if the body were woven as a single fabric of piezoelectric collagen fibres, producing a continual energetic flow of data thru the electronic fabric," said Dr James Oschman[2].

This information supports our ability to make physical changes. It appears the crystal like energetic activity aids the process of healing and self-regulation.

Your body is continually seeking balance and health. Given the right conditions it has the capacity to self-regulate and heal. We see this when we cut ourselves. The wonderful process of repair that occurs cannot be replicated by science. Your body has an intelligence all of its own and exactly how it repairs remains a mystery.

We do know that as long as you are alive energy is flowing through your system. Vitality is determined by the frequency, quantity and quality of that energy flow. As well as the degree to which your Chakras are open. When you make a paradigm shift and use skills like Energy Exercises for managing energy, you will always have an abundance of energy for life.

Benefits of Energy Exercise

Vitality and high energy levels are just some of the benefits of incorporating Energy Exercises into your daily life. We all know more exercise is good, some of us love it while others avoid it at all costs, which is not wise! Well Energy Exercises are not the no pain no gain variety, they don't require lots of energy to do. They give you energy.

Energy Exercises are designed to raise your energetic frequency and quality of energy as well as build your energy resources and get more energy flowing through your chakras. As well as detoxing and charging your system on the energetic level they also have what my teacher called side effects. These are all the physiological and psychological benefits such as:

Physiological

- Enhancing the circulation, purifying your body and speeding up the removal of toxins
- Increasing oxygen supply to your lungs and consequently all your cells and organs.
- Increasing lung capacity thus creating greater respiratory efficiency
- Reducing stress and tension in your muscles and connective tissues
- Massaging your internal organs, increasing immune function and flushing out waste products and toxins
- Improving posture and developing greater body awareness and self image
- Helping to balance and stabilize the autonomic nervous system, creating a state of equilibrium.

Psychological

- Concentration and focus improves
- Inducing the relaxation response
- Building body awareness and sense of self
- Attention and depth of perception increases
- Non competitive, encouraging you to enjoy the process rather than worrying about the end goal
- Feeling happier due to improved hormone balance, especially serotonin, dopamine and endorphin levels.

- Energy Exercises are a great anti-depressant!
- High achievement and satisfaction levels.

Taking time to introduce a few Energy Exercises into your daily routine will have you feeling good and looking good in no time. That's the beauty of them – you can feel the results immediately as they work on the energetic level creating ease and balance in the body, mind, spirit continuum. The gentle continuous movements penetrate the subatomic level uniting body, mind and spirit.

As you become mindful and allow your breath to tune with the movements, you enter a parasympathetic dominant space, where self-regulation, healing and pain reduction can occur. This mindful state of, conscious emptiness is often referred to as presence. A peaceful yet alert inner space where energy and consciousness are raised and spirit truly embodied. Energy Exercises encourage you to empty your mind, relax your body and be present in the moment. It seems the more space we can create in our systems, the more energy we invite in.

Power Half Hour

So how do we practice Energy Exercises? My suggestion is creating what I call a Power Half Hour. This is a time in the morning and/or evening where you make space for you alone or for your family where you create an Energy Exercise session. Sessions are created to stimulate the energy system in the morning and relax in the evening. The greatest benefits are achieved through regular daily practice. E4L Practitioners recommend and teach a number of Energy Exercises, some of which I introduce below. Energy Exercises are always conducted with ease.

In yoga it's known as *inaction in action,* or wu wei in chi gong. The idea is to work with your body, not to over work it. They are Energy Exercises not purely mechanical exercises. They each relate to chakras and elements and I categorize them accordingly below. Energy Exercises are safe and easy to learn. They are powerful and energizing for all ages, sizes and genders. I think of them as anytime, anywhere exercises. That might be stretching it a bit. But I have certainly been seen in airports, planes and parks doing Energy Exercises. Start at home and judge for yourself.

General – To awaken all chakras and elements

Energy4life Balance

This balance can be used to begin and end Energy Exercise sessions. It releases the body's natural tranquilizers, helping to calm your body and focus the mind. It also cultivates self love.

Use your hands to channel energy through your body and chakras.

Your right hand has a positive charge and gives energy.

Your left hand has a negative charge and receives energy.

- Take a few moments to relax by deepening your breath. Make yourself comfortable lying down with your feet separated and your palms facing up, alongside your body or sit upright with your legs crossed.

- Gently place your right hand over your Heart chakra and your left hand over your Sacral chakra. Breathe deeply allowing energy to flow between your hands. Close your eyes and feel a sense of calm emerging. Relax and re-balance your energy.

- As you breathe sense love flowing from your Heart chakra to your Sacral chakra, allow the calming energy of love to bring balance to every cell of your body. Release anything that no longer serves you, tension, pain, disharmony, let it all go and fill your entire system with loving life giving energy. Know that Divine love is your very essence.

- This balance draws on an infinite supply of universal love and compassion at your Heart chakra. By placing your right hand (giving) over your Heart chakra and your left hand (receiving) over your Sacral chakra you are drawing an abundance of universal loving energy from your heart into your Sacral chakra. The Sacral chakra is the sacred home of I. This balance sends love from you to you. A great exercise for developing self love.

This exercise can be used by all. It's popular with children and great for teaching them how to self-soothe and calm their energy when fearful or worried. You can also use this balance with family and friends to help them relax. Practitioners can also use this technique with clients.

Mountain Pose – Standing Alignment

This is a fundamental standing posture in yoga. Here we use it to align the body encouraging increased energy flow.

- Stand with you feet hip distance apart, toes slightly turned in heels slightly out.

- Lengthen your whole body, pulling up on your knee caps opening your pelvis, lengthen your spine, open your chest and across your shoulders, allowing your arms to relax at your sides.

- Lengthen the back of your neck by tipping your chin slightly forward and lifting from the top of your head. Gaze directly ahead and then gently close your eyes.

- Elevate your whole body, opening every cell and breathing deeply to oxygenate your whole system. Feel that you are taking up space in your body. Root your feet firmly to our mother the earth and reach up spreading your upper body towards the sun. Feel your entire body alive and charged with energy.

- This simple posture develops body awareness and increases body image. It re-aligns your system creating more space for your internal organs to function and energy to flow. It is a powerful posture in itself and is also used as a starting pose for other exercises.

- Hold the posture for two minutes with awareness, listening to your energy.

Energy Spiral

This is a standing spinal twist that can be used to activate your chakras and Energy Field.

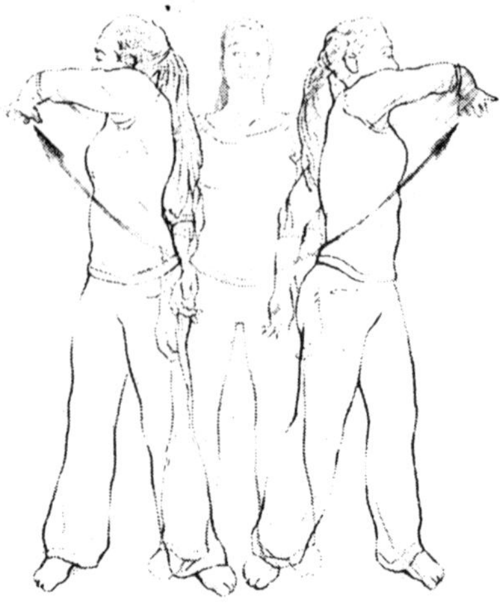

- Stand in mountain pose with your feet slightly turned out and body upright.
  Take some deep breaths.

- Gently begin to twist from right to left, keep your feet firm and your arms floppy. Bend your knees in rhythm and allow your arms to float up as you spiral around. Let your arms float up towards your head and slowly back down to the Root chakra with each movement. Gently spiralling energy up and down your chakras. Continue for a few minutes then gently slow your movement to a place of stillness.

- Breathe deeply, listening carefully to your energy as it flows through your system. Repeat exercise three times.

- This exercise awakens and activates the spinal nerves and circulatory system, lubricating the spine and warming the body.

- The Energy Spiral works with the centripetal and centrifugal forces of nature. These are electromagnetic fields that rise and fall through and around every single atom. Centripetal is the inward flow of energy and centrifugal the outward flow. It also works to stimulate the double helix caduceus currents. *"From the whirling galaxies above to the spinning atoms below, all creation is a spiral helix"*.

- Tapping into the spiralling energy and then becoming still draws energy into your creative core centre. It resonates with the power that weaves matter from pure consciousness. Use daily to energise all your Chakras and awaken your body.

Hand Energy Sensing – a great meditative exercise that you can use daily to awaken energy and develop overall awareness and deep relaxation. Details are in chapter one.

Air Energy

Ocean Breath

This calming practice fully utilizes your breathing apparatus and expands lung capacity. It is named after the rolling waves of the ocean.

- Make yourself comfortable lying down with your feet separated and your palms facing up alongside your body. Let go of any tightness and tension. Relax your whole body and bring attention to your breath. Place one hand over your lower abdomen.

- Breathe in fully through your nose, raising your abdomen for a count of four. Open your chest completely feeling the wavelike movement of your lungs as they fill. (Your hand should lift upwards).

- Hold your breath comfortably, keeping the body totally still for a count of four.

- Slowly exhale through your nose for a count of four emptying your lungs completely. Feel your abdomen pulling down towards the floor as you breathe. (Your hand will be lowered).

Repeat the Ocean Breath three to seven times, increasing the count with practice.

This exercise allows full and correct use of the breathing apparatus. It restores movement to the diaphragm and intercostal muscles. Five times more oxygen enters the lungs and is transported around your body's cells. This flushes out toxins, relaxes the nervous system and improves concentration.

The ability to control your breath is fundamental to spiritual development.

Caution: people with back problems may wish to lay down with knees raised and feet placed flat on the floor in front of the buttocks.

Diaphragm Release

This exercise releases tension in the diaphragm freeing up old dormant emotions and opening the gateway between the personal and universal chakras.

- The diaphragm is a large umbrella shaped muscle that separates the thoracic and abdominal cavities. Like all muscles it can get very tense.

- Kneel down sitting on your feet if possible, if not this can be done in a chair. Align your spine and take a few deep breaths to open your lungs. Find your diaphragm by gently tracing your fingers along the edge of your ribcage.

- Now place your fingers on the outer edge of your ribcage,

raise your spine breathe in and exhale as you go forward. Your fingers will begin to go under your ribcage applying pressure to the diaphragm. Inhale and come up. Now walk your fingers slightly towards the centre and repeat – raise your spine breathe in and exhale as you go all the way forward. Continue this several times until your fingers are at the centre – your sternum and solar plexus area.

- This is a powerful exercise and working with the breath is essential. You can go deeper with each breath, being mindful of any tension or discomfort. Finish with your spine upright. Listening to your energy. Repeat exercise three times.

On a physical level the diaphragm release frees up any trapped gas and tension in the abdominal region encouraging energy to flow. It also opens the energy pathways passing through the diaphragm enhancing energy movement between the lower and higher chakras. This is an important transition point in the human energy system.

Caution: The conscious breathing and pressure can awaken stagnant emotions, fear and pain. This energy could have been around since childhood. So be gentle with this exercise.

The Cat and Variations

This is quite a well known Energy Exercise, influenced by the movement of cats as they stretch. It brings more energy and flexibility to the spine, so can be very healing.

Begin on all fours, knees hip width apart, hands shoulder width apart and feet directly behind your knees. This should create a stable posture. Begin by breathing nice and deeply.

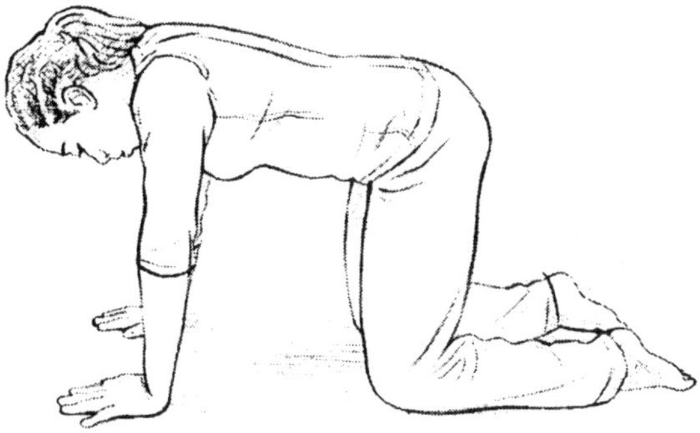

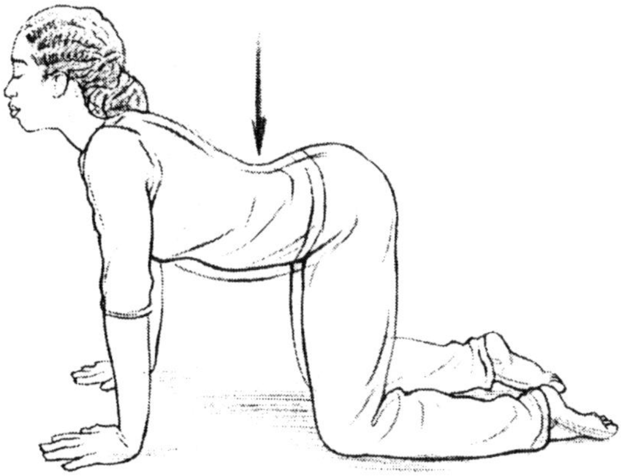

- Then introduce the spinal curve. Inhale dipping your spine and raise your head and your tail. (Your coccyx is a residual tail.)

- As you exhale, reverse the movement arching your spine

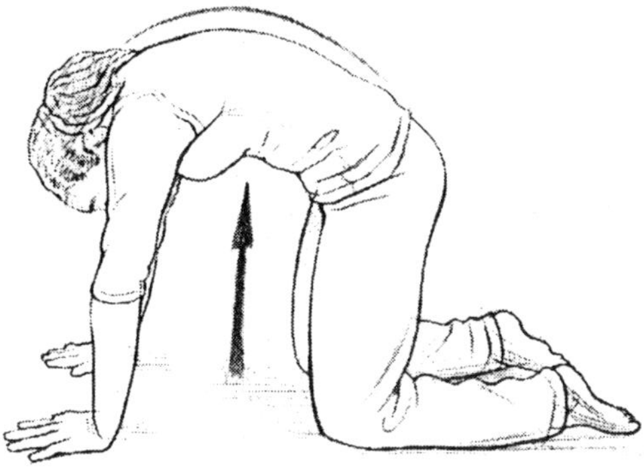

tucking in your head and your tail. Come back to neutral and repeat three to seven times. Make sure your breathing is deep and your stretch extensive.

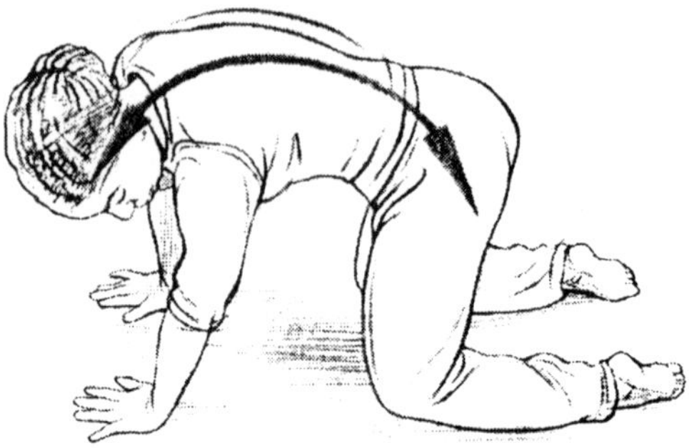

- Variation - breathe in pull your waist towards the right and your head and tail towards the left. Then reverse, waist to the left, head and tail right. Come back to centre. Repeat. This works your waist, oblique muscles and abdominal organs.

You know how flexible and agile cats are. This is their secret. Keep the spine and consequently the nerves that feed the whole body flexible and healthy. A healthy spine equals a healthy body and a healthy body equals long life.

Fire Energy

Wood Chopper

The Wood Chopper is a great way to release anger, frustration and negative fire energy. It also has a stimulating effect that warms the system and builds a sense of confidence and assertion.

The Wood Chopper is simple but powerful, so start slowly and build a rhythm that will gently warm up your body.

- Position your feet slightly wider than hip width apart with your knees slightly bent. Inhale, expand your chest, clasp your hands and raise your arms up above your head. From this position, exhale and swing down as if chopping wood. Slowly raise yourself back up and repeat as many times as feels comfortable for you. Use a loud **ha!** sound each time you go forward.

When you've finished this exercise be still for a moment and feel the movement of energy flowing through your body. The Wood Chopper is fun and releases tension in your whole body. It transforms anger and frustration into laughter and joy. It's great for children.

Caution: Avoid this exercise if you have lower back pain.

Six Pointed Star – Balances Fire and Water

A gentle balancing exercise, that works with Heart chakra energy uniting the masculine and feminine energies in the body. It

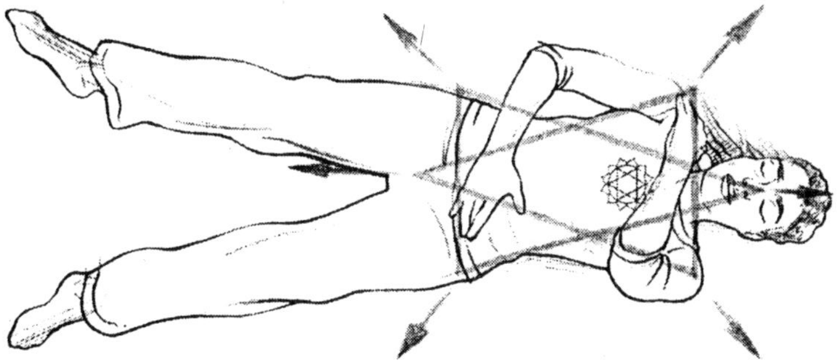

helps you embody the life of spirit and free the life of your body.

- Start by lying on the floor in the relaxation pose, feet separated and falling out to the sides, palms facing up, alongside your body. Breathe deeply. You could use the Ocean Breath.

- Now take your attention to your Heart chakra. The symbol for this chakra is a six pointed star, two interlaced triangles. One apex reaches up towards the sky; this represents the feminine water energy and the personal chakras. The downward pointing triangle represents masculine fire energy and universal chakras.

- In your mind's eye visualize your Heart chakra and the six pointed star centred in your body. Tune to the energy of balance and unity. Now imagine the star expanding, opening out and embracing your body, feel your body centred and relaxed inside the star pattern. You become the centre of the expansive star.

- Now you can place your hands on six points of your body, representing six points of the star. Place your right hand on left shoulder, left hand on right hip, gently open diagonally as if pulling your hands apart, without using any pressure only energy. Then take your left hand to right shoulder, right hand to left hip and open energetically. Then create the final two points by placing right fingertips over your Brow chakra and the left fingertips over your pubic bone. Breathe and energetically extend and open.

- Rest your hands by your sides, palms up. In your mind's eye, draw the six pointed star back in to your Heart chakra. Breathe as your body fully expands and opens. Feel yourself relaxed, rebalanced and open to spirit. Energy freely coursing through your body. Be still and listen. This is a powerful polarity balance. Working with the forces of involution - spirit into matter and evolution – matter returning to spirit. It is deeply relaxing, healing, and transformational.

Water Energy

Deviasana - Goddess Pose

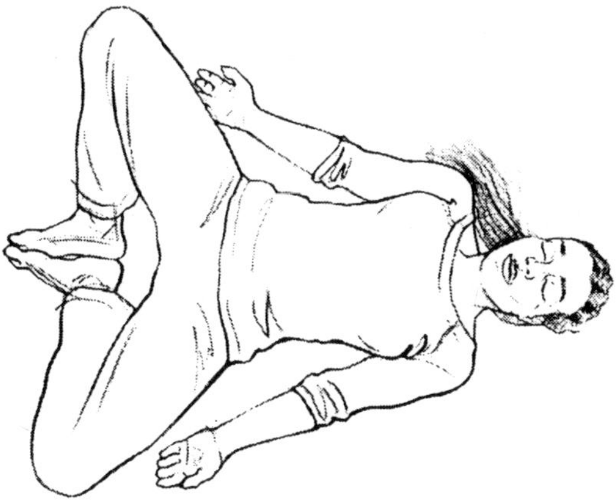

This is a calming exercise that allows energy to flow through the pelvis. It activates water energy cleansing the pelvic bowl and all its organs.

- Lie on your back with your legs stretched out. Bring your heels towards your pelvis, put the soles of your feet together and let your knees fall out to the sides. Relax in this pose, allowing energy to flow freely through the pelvis into the legs and from the legs into the pelvis.

- Enjoy the sensation as energy floods into your pelvis. Breathe deeply in through your nose and out through your pelvis/genitals. Hold the posture for five minutes or as long as is comfortable for you. Then relax with your legs stretched out.

This exercise allows energy to flow freely through the pelvis, activating any stagnant water. Keeping energy flowing in the pelvic waters is vital for prevention of ovarian, testicular, cervical and prostate cancers; plus all ailments of the womb and pelvis. It also keeps sexual energy flowing and restores vitality to the pelvic area.

Earth Energy

Pyramid and Variations

This standing posture stimulates the spine and nervous system. It also strengthens the thighs and arms as well as opening the pelvis and shoulders. It's a great energizer for the whole body.

- Stand with feet wide apart and facing outwards. Lean forwards placing your hands just above your knees, thumbs on the inside. Knees are directly over your ankles.

Now lengthen your spine and straighten your arms, shoulders are up towards your ears. Breathe deeply and let your neck relax. This posture stretches your whole body. Return to standing and repeat three times.

- Variations. You can rock gently, breathing deeply and rhythmically. You can also twist your spine and torso to the right, looking over right shoulder, arms straight and hips low. Repeat, twisting to your left side. This exercise releases tension in the spine, you may hear it cracking.

This wide legged squatting posture is known as the 'youth pose' as it keeps the body strong and healthy into old age if practiced daily. All systems in the body are activated and energy flow accelerated. Be gentle but firm with yourself. Remember to practice inaction in action.

Child pose

This is a resting posture. The body enfolds drawing energy to the core. Following the natural rhythm of expansion and contraction

this contractive pose can be done after an expansive exercise like the Pyramid.

- Kneel down and sit on your heels, place your hands palms upwards alongside your feet, slowly exhale as you bend forward bringing your chest to your thighs, forehead to the floor. Breathe and relax, holding the posture for 2-5 minutes.
- The Child pose stretches the lower back relieving any compression or pain. It gently stretches the pelvis, thighs, calves and ankles. It also calms the system relieving fatigue and headaches. Energy is drawn into the internal organs as the parasympathetic nervous system is stimulated. A yin exercise quietly connecting you to the earth our mother.

Energy Exercises can be used individually, working with the elements to enhance energy levels or you can create a sequence. Try starting with the Energy4life Balance follow with a breathing exercise, like the Ocean Breath then a stretch such as the Cat or Pyramid. End by gently slowing down with the Six Pointed Star Balance.

Use Energy Exercise mindfully, work slowly with awareness, stopping to feel the energy moving through your body. Be at home in your physical vehicle and fully embody spirit. Experience your body as a Divine gift from the Creator and invite energy to flow freely through you. Restore, revitalise and heal your body. Listen carefully as energy flows; for within each movement and wave of energy is a message. Honor and love your sacred body temple. Give thanks for each breath and the life that moves you.

Chapter Six

Energy Psychology – Values, Beliefs and Lifescripts

Destiny is not a matter of chance
it is a matter of choice,
it is not to be waited for
it is to be created.

What is Energy Psychology?

Psychology is an ever-changing science. One of its recent incarnations is positive psychology, which is an attempt to look on the bright side of human behavior and focus on what makes us happy, rather than on crisis management and what is wrong. The findings of positive psychology coincide with many spiritual teachings such as *thought power* in the yoga tradition and *mindfulness* in Buddhism. These spiritual teachings were created to help us positively use the magnificent resource of mind.

Positive psychology takes us in the direction of happiness and fulfilment, a welcome shift. However when we take a step further, we meet Energy Psychology the most recent incarnation on the journey. What pleases me about Energy Psychology is its apparent return to the original meaning of the word psychology.

Psychology explores how we think, feel and behave. Yet when we look at the origins of the word psychology from the Greek *psyche* it translates as breath, spirit, soul and *logia* meaning study of. So we have the study of breath, spirit, soul. These newer avenues of psychology offer a welcome addition to more established routes. Overall Psychology seeks to study and therefore better understand the psyche.

In E4L we draw from both Ancient and contemporary

knowledge of the psyche and its workings. We recognize that everything is energy, energy is all there is. It is the power behind all things and no-thing. The E4L system uses Energy Psychology to explore the energy behind our thoughts, feelings and actions. We look at the values that drive us, the beliefs that shape us and the scripts we live by. The aim is to release stress, increase energy flow and free the mind. Energy Psychology is all about releasing what you don't need, transforming the energy and embracing life's abundant blessings.

Energy Economy

How much energy do you have invested in holding on to negative energy that no longer serves you? What obstacles are in the way of your success? Are you allowing yourself to procrastinate? Are there habits and patterns in your life past their sell-by date, maybe even people? Are you ready for change?

I think it is safe to say we all seek happiness. No-one truly enjoys the pain and struggle of life, although sometimes we do get stuck and choose to linger on the negative side. After all life is a series of choices, from the moment you wake up to the moment you fall asleep again you are making choices. Those choices determine your destiny. You are programming your destiny every minute of every day. You are not only living in the moment you are also creating your future. Every thought, choice of food, attitude and action determines your future. You are only reading this book now because you thought about it previously. It only exists because I chose to write it. Remember *today is the tomorrow you dreamed about yesterday.* It is all a matter of choice. Are you choosing to live consciously? Are you choosing more energy for your life? In E4L I simply cut to the core by asking the power question. *How do you use or abuse your energy and how could you use it better?*

This laser question zones in on the energy. Since we know everything is made from energy. It makes sense to ask, how are you using your valuable resource? It's energy economy. Do you still have some week left at the end of your energy? Do you find yourself lacking in energy, drained, exhausted and stressed out all the time? Is something not quite adding up? Do you lack what you need most and have a little too much of what you don't need.

If this is your experience, or any other variation, then it's time to think about energy, consciousness and change. It's time to shift your thinking, release any sluggish, moribund energy and choose a high energy life. Improving your energy economy is easier than you may think. Let's look at some basics of psychology from a spiritual perspective.

Layers of the Psyche

Below I outline three layers of the psyche. The persona is the self or mask we show the world. When someone asks "how are you" the persona may say "I am fine", regardless of what is happening on a deeper level. The middle layer, the armoring is made up of the unconscious mind, our protective defences, fears and conflicts. It is from here that our perceptions and individual reality is often created or certainly influenced. The world we see is tainted by our own pathology. And nestled in the very center is our core energy. The spirit, our infinite potential, that which is always evolving and unfolding into greater being.

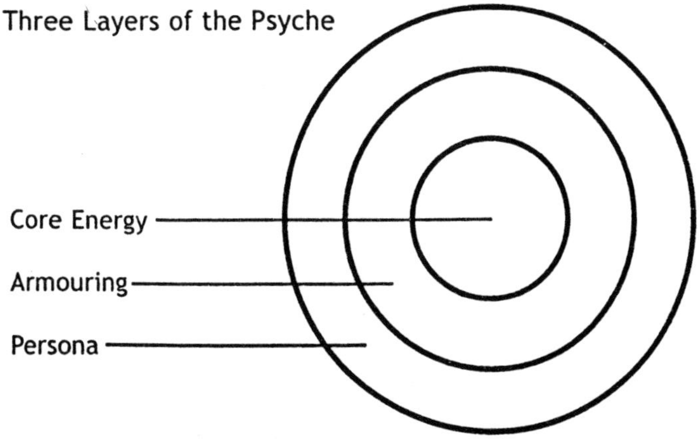

The middle layer is particularly complex and contractive. It can store a lifetime of fearful and painful memories. It holds our beliefs about the world, our values in life and the stories we live by. This is where we create drama, rehearsing scripts in which we play the leading role. This layer often holds us back, preventing energy flowing freely between the optimistic core and the dangerously perceived world.

I coached a client, Sarah[1], who told me about the pain of her divorce and her worries about how this might affect her children. But it wasn't only her children, she also felt guilty about not spending enough time with her ageing parents. Plus she was under pressure at work and in the midst of all this Sarah really wanted a new direction in her life. So she was studying at home to become a nutritionist. Sarah was so tired, angry and resentful. She shared with me that she felt negative about her life and everyone in it. Sarah was allowing life to really get her down. With more energy going out than coming in, she had got into serious energy debt! Her energy levels were low and restricted in the middle layer.

The problem that arises when armoring limits energy flow, is that we can get used to the restriction, and worse still addicted to the many layers of chaos and drama in our lives. There are numerous chemicals flooding through our bodies all the time, a veritable inner pharmacy. And according to pharmacologist and research scientist Candace Pert, we can get addicted to these chemicals. For example Sarah's anger created a specific chemical signature in her body, and each time she got angry she became more familiar with the chemical signature and needed to find things to get angry about in order to create an inner chemical fix. It's not only anger that triggers these chemical reactions and subsequent addictions it can be other emotions as well. Candace Pert talks about molecules of emotion and her work explains how we get addicted to the internal chemicals our life dramas create.

In a healthy system, energy flows freely from the positive life affirming core out into the world. Energy can also return freely carrying feedback from the world into our deepest core. Ultimately we want energy to flow unrestricted by our armoring. That is not to say that our defences are totally negative, on the contrary they are part of our ability to self regulate and survive in a sometimes hostile world. It only becomes a problem when flexibility is lost and fears are expressed inappropriately. It becomes negative when it no longer serves us. A child may need to hold energy back to prevent pain, whereas an adult may need to develop confidence and deal with the source of the pain. In Sarah's case that meant communicating with some of the people involved.

Holding back prevents energy flowing from the core. This can be a problem because and the core holds our richness. It is the seat of our inner beauty, creativity and higher potential. All the good stuff is waiting to be expressed from your expansive core. Answers to life's many questions can be found there. It is also from this layer that we connect with that which is greater than us. Some call it God, Energy, Great Spirit, Inner Power. It is the force that causes the sun to rise, rain to fall and the resulting creation of life. When you cut yourself it directs the healing, when a sperm and egg meet it weaves new life. That indescribable yet knowable energy resides in your core. It is your very essence.

Mindfulness, meditation and spiritual practices are designed solely to facilitate the process of knowing this essence of who you are. Developing presence allows you to tap into what I call the Ongoing Evolutionary Process OEP. This is the ever evolving consciousness, core energy expressing itself from the centre of your being. The god intelligence, that moves through around and as you. The G.O.D. the Gift Of Divinity that is constantly calling you into greater alignment, purpose, passion and peace.

Put simply, energy is continually unfolding and when we tune into this evolving spiritual/causal layer it completely shifts our perceptions and expands our consciousness freeing our infinite potential to be fully expressed. Energy is a constantly evolving infinite resource. We are the energy and intelligence that created the universe. When we tap into this level of our consciousness we become co-creators and powerful vessels of creation and change. We have all experienced amazing things happening when we are connected to our centre and in the flow. Sound good! You know it is. So what happens, why don't we always feel connected and in the flow? In most cases somewhere along the line, we learn that it is not safe to allow energy to flow freely.

Values, Beliefs and Life Scripts

In various ways we develop protective patterns and limiting beliefs. We create stories, dramas that we repeatedly play on the big screen in our minds. We take scenarios and characters from the past and give them new roles in our futures. Then we glorify and justify the script, so far it's all fiction, but we believe it and act as if it is real.

Your mind is so powerful. It works for you 24 hours a day, every day of your life. You talk to yourself more than anyone else speaks to you. What are you thinking and saying? Is your self-talk positive and encouraging? Or do you find yourself using terms like, it's just not me, I can't, it's too late, there's never enough, I'm too fat, I'm broke, I could never, life is hard, etc, etc. Limiting beliefs and judgemental self-talk can zap energy in a big way.

Your mind believes everything you say. *Whether you say you can or you say you can't, you are always right.* So why use unconstructive, negative self talk? If the way you talk to yourself is anything other than positive and encouraging you are wasting time and precious energy. Change the script, sing a different tune, fake it till you make it, whatever it takes, make sure the way you speak to yourself is the way you would speak to a valued friend. We are shaped by the voices we hear in our own heads. This needn't be a problem. When we live consciously we can use positive self-talk to support our values. In order to do this we need to know our values. What is really important to you? And how much of your time and energy do you spend on your chief values? One way to see what is really important is looking in your diary and cheque book. What/who do you spend most of your time and money on? Another way is to do a simple values elicitation exercise[2].

Values Elicitation Exercise

This is useful to do with a partner or small group. It's easier to come up with a longer initial list of values.

1. You will need your journal and a pen. Start by listing all the values that are important to you. List as many as you can. Ask yourself what values do I feel strongly about? Create a list or mind map. It may look something like this.

Extended Values List			
Leadership	Kindness	Gratitude	Empowerment
Determination	Honesty	Enthusiasm	Acceptance
Recognition	Mastery	Freedom	Self-expression
Love	Clarity	Mindfulness	Teamwork
Wealth	Optimism	Health	Playfulness
Pleasure	Articulacy	Happiness	Focus
Wisdom	Courage	Spirituality	Achievement
Justice	Passion	Tranquillity	Self-discipline
Peace	Excellence	Integrity	Learning
Creativity	Humility	Humour	Compassion

2. Choose 10-15 values from your list that are most important and make a second list

3. Then arrange them in order of personal priority
4. Now you can see your top ten values.
5. Finally ask yourself if your self-talk supports your values?

Bringing your values into your conscious mind can support the choices you make by providing greater clarity and focus. This allows you to consciously live in alignment with what is closest to your heart. So keep them near, as a reminder of what is really important. Whenever you have a difficult decision to make, a major life change or someone threatens your stability refer to your top ten values. Ask yourself how would someone with these values think and behave in this situation?

Health and happiness were high on Sarah's value list and spirituality. Yet they didn't figure high in her life. Things began to change as a result of the work we did together. The mind is very powerful but often it works overtime and we need to get out of the head and into the body. One of our first steps was inviting Sarah back into her body. Drama is very *he did – she did – it's not my fault*. It requires a lot of thinking and mind games. So in order to experience something deeper in life, we have to press the mute button and start to feel the sensations in the body. We have to deepen the breath and simply enjoy being alive. Despite all that has happened. You are still here. So give thanks.

At the heart of E4L is spiritual practice. When Sarah started practising her daily Energy Exercises and meditation she started to take control of her life again. Then we could start exploring her beliefs. Like many people much of Sarah's thinking was negative, unconstructive and untrue. Fortunately Sarah was conscious of that and sought change.

Beliefs

Our beliefs shape our reality. Beliefs are energy lifting or energy depleting, depending on how you choose to think. What we believe often shows up in the stories we tell. I was told as a child that I could do anything I put my mind to. I still believe it. As a teenager, after witnessing a classmate declare she was *so depressed,* I decided never to get depressed, and so far I haven't. I have had my low points in life, but I never apply the term depression to myself. I believe it helps me recover quicker. I believe that no matter what happens in life, all is well. Most of the traumatic and painful things in my life happened in childhood so I believe that life unfolds and gets better. These are some beliefs I am aware of. Beliefs operate from the conscious and unconscious mind, all affecting our behaviour. What are some of the beliefs you live by?

The good thing about beliefs is they don't actually need to be true; they simply need to empower you. The beliefs you hold are the rules you live by; rules that influence your behaviour. Ideally they should serve you positively. However some beliefs are limiting, outdated, trapped in the middle layer of our armouring, doing nothing to move us forward. These are the ones we need to release and let go. You can choose to rewrite the script at anytime. You are the director of your own life. You can shift your worldview, change your thinking and you change your life. Remember it's all choices that we make, stories we tell and destiny we create. What do you want to believe?

Identifying Limiting Beliefs

In your journal or below, write down three beliefs you live by that really support you.

1. ______________________________

2. ______________________________

3. ______________________________

Now list how they make you feel.

____

____

____

____

Write three beliefs that limit you and hold you back.

1. ______________________________________

2. ______________________________________

3. ______________________________________

How does this feel?

____

____

____

____

____

____

Have you identified any beliefs that are past their sell by date, outdated scripts that no longer serve you, beliefs you want to release? Sometimes we hold onto things that don't belong to us, beliefs about past hurts and pains, feelings of worthlessness, shame, anger, thoughts of revenge. We believe we deserve the wrong relationship, addictions, jobs that no longer meet our creative needs. We may hold beliefs that create negative attitudes, judgments about ourselves or others. When a belief no longer serves you, let it go. When you have more energy holding you back than moving you forward it is time to release and let go.

Energy Release Technique™

I developed the Energy Release Technique ™ (ERT) as part of the E4L programme. It's a self help tool that is also used with clients by E4L Coaches. It's a simple yet powerful way of releasing anything that no longer serves you. It works at the quantum level, releasing obstructions and interference patterns that prevent free flowing energy.

My background is psychotherapeutic bodywork and for many years I worked with people releasing issues that literally get stuck in their tissues. The body is made up of biological tissue, muscle tissue, nerve tissue, and connective tissue. Research[3] is beginning to show what the Ancients have told us and what I experience as a body therapist, that the body has a unique intelligence. The physical body has memory. Your cells, your muscles and nerves hold information. This is known as cellular memory. The cells in your body store emotional trauma from landmarks and incidents in your life, like severe shocks, heartbreaks, rejections, abuse, loss, separation, accidents, surgery, pain, anger, fear, low self esteem a lifetimes wounding and emotional hurt can get lodged in your physical body. These memories create energetic contractions that interfere with full expansive energy flow. See below some of the ways emotional states can affect the physical body.

Emotion/Feeling	Energy restricted in Chakra and related body part
Anger	Energy restricted in the Solar Plexus chakra and digestive system
Anxiety	Energy restricted in Sacral chakra pelvic area and adrenals
Depression	Energy restricted in Heart chakra, shoulders and arms
Fear	Energy restricted in Root chakra legs, feet, knees
Grief	Energy restricted in Throat chakra, spine, voice box
Loneliness	Energy restricted in Heart and Sacral chakras, chest and pelvis
Low self-esteem	Energy restricted in Sacral and Throat chakras, communication problems
Pain	Energy restricted in Heart chakra, causing problems in whole body
Panic attacks	Energy restricted in Root chakra, Heart chakra, can't move, can't breathe
Sadness	Energy restricted in Heart chakra, Sacral chakra, affects sense of self.

Memories held in our tissues can restrict the flow of energy and limit our capacity to live fully expressed lives. These energy restrictions can also lead to physical illnesses or as Carolyn Myss puts it; *your biography becomes your biology*.

I developed ERT to release interference and restrictions in the tissue. This allows energy to be transformed on a cellular level and an expansive rhythm to be re-established in the energy field. ERT is a gentle way to melt pain, trauma and release energy that is trapped in the middle layer. We simply need to be ready to let go of painful armour. These defensive emotions drain energy and hold us back. We need to be willing to let go of the destructive, blaming, disempowering scripts.

Sarah started out very angry, blaming her husband for everything. She thought it was entirely his fault. She experienced a lot of grief and loss after the divorce. She felt he had let her and the children down, leaving them all vulnerable and fearful. The release technique supported Sarah to let go of the scripts, attitudes and behaviors that were causing her pain.

The more I use the release technique the more I see just how quickly and effectively people can embrace change when working at the energy level. Energy operates on the quantum brain where change can happen instantly. The change we thought took years of analysis, we are now witnessing in minutes. Tapping into the core energy level allows change to happen in an instant if we allow it, it is the resistance to change that takes time.

Think about it you are changing anyway, *change is the only constant*. Every cell in your body is changing as you read. You are older now than when you started reading the page, you are on a one way journey towards life's end. Cells are dying, being maintained and growing anew. Change is taking place, you are learning as you read, new synapses are being created in your brain. You are no longer as you were five minutes ago, you have changed.

When we start to live consciously we recognise the OEP - ongoing evolutionary process. We know we are constantly changing and we decide how we want to change, how we want to programme our destiny, how we want to live life to the full in every moment with fully expressive and expansive energy coursing through us. This is your choice. You can hold onto old energy that doesn't feel good or you can let it go. We have the technology to tap into the quantum energetic level and create instant change.

Sarah chose E4L because she wanted to let go, she wanted to release the anger and the pain that was killing her. She realised that her energy and her moods were negatively affecting her children. She reached a point where she was ready to let it all go and move on with her life. We used the ERT outlined below and she also received Energy Alignment from me to facilitate internal balance.

The Energy Release Technique is powerful because

1. It provides a tool, a resource anyone can use on themselves.
2. There is no need to retell the stories and relive the trauma, it not necessary.
3. The technique can be used anytime and anywhere, there is no tapping required as in some similar techniques
4. It works on a quantum level creating change instantly.
5. It provides an opportunity to transform trapped energy and embrace life's many blessings.

It takes a lot of energy to hold onto negative feelings and old hurts. When this energy is released and transformed it becomes available to use in constructive ways that fuel and advance life in the direction of your dreams. It allows you to tap into the OEP and ask "What is my soul purpose in life?" "Why am I here and what am I really being asked to do?"

Your daily practice then becomes a time for deep reflection, opening to spirit and listening as the universe speaks through you. When you take time to be still, amazing sensations can be experienced within the watery depths of your being. You can touch your true essence and meet your higher self. You can tap into a power, an energy that is constantly flowing through and around you.

Eckhart Tolle says "*You are here to allow the Divine Purpose of the universe to unfold. That's how important you are.*"[4]

Before him, wise people and sages of old shared this

knowledge. We are here for a Purpose, a Divine Purpose. Buddhists call this Dharma. No direct translation in English, but generally it means *holding our true essence.* I think of it as *living life on purpose,* living in a way that elevates your body, mind and spirit. Dharma not drama!

Energy Release Technique Protocol[5]

This powerful tool frees up negative energy and restores energy flow. It can be done standing or sitting allowing you to move easily if necessary. You simply tap into the energy and release it. Free flowing energy is essential for health and wellbeing. ERT aims to restore energy flow and freedom to your bodymind. Follow steps one to ten.

1. Is there anything that you would like to let go of, any feelings, anger, shame, fear. Old beliefs, I am not good enough, I can't, I never.... Outdated scripts like: it's not for me, I am too scared to.... Old habits, panicking, worrying, anything that no longer serves you that you want to release? Are you ready to work on it now? If your answer is yes, let's go!

2. We know from quantum physics that change can happen in an instant. It is resistance to change that takes time.

3. Take a moment to clarify what you are holding, a feeling, emotion, script (there is no need to tell anyone)

4. On a scale of 1 – 10 how much energy does holding it take?
   1 – very little   10 - a lot

5. Where do you feel the emotion in your body? Go inside to that place now. Touch it with your hands. Describe how it

looks and feels? What is the quality is it heavy, dense, thick or sticky? Does it have a colour? Sometimes you may feel it but not see it or vice versa. It's all energy and it's all fine.

6. It is **ONLY ENERGY** – everything is only energy

7. Now invite the energy interference to release, simply say the words **release and flow.** Allow energy to flow and observe its movement through your body's natural energy channels. You may want to stroke or pull the energy out.

8. Track the energy, where does it want to go? Allow energy to move until it finds an exit point. This can be anywhere on your body. Hands, feet, head or any other place. Continue repeating quietly or out loud the words **release and flow.**

9. How does that feel? It is possible for it to be completely released. Results can take place very quickly. (So quickly sometimes that it's hard to believe.)

10. On a scale of 1-10 how does the energy feel now?

11. You can continue or repeat the exercise at another time until you reach 1 or 0.

12. To finish, remember this simple but powerful tool can be used anywhere and anytime you choose to release emotions and the energy restrictions they create.

Complete by using the **Energy4Life Balance** to relax and calm your system.

The results are immediate you can feel the energy shift.

Energy is now available to be re-channelled in constructive ways. Ask yourself the following questions and enter a quiet meditative space to receive the answers.

- What is the universe offering me right now?
- What opportunities are being presented to me?
- What must I be or do to enter into alignment with my highest good?

Remember Energy Psychology is all about letting go of what you don't need, transforming the energy and embracing lives abundant blessings.

Stepping up and Stepping out

It is time for you to connect with the OEP and embrace your blessings. Is it time for you to step up and step out in the world? We each have a unique and important role to play in life, like a giant jigsaw puzzle each piece is equally important and has its own place. If just one piece of the puzzle is unavailable, it will be missed. No other piece can take its place. Each piece has a responsibility to the whole. We each have our place in it, all equally important and if you do not show up, no one can take your place.

If you have work to do, no-one else can do it for you. I am the only person to write *this* book. Gabrielle Roth the only person to create the five rhythms, Van Gogh is the only artist to paint in his style, Gandhi was the one to initiate and lead peaceful protest in India, Oprah is the one to create the Oprah show, Obama is the only leader inspiring hope in his way, at this time.

Everyone had to step up and step out. No-one told anyone to do it, you just know in your heart. It doesn't matter how big or small from writing a book to leading the world. If that's your piece of the puzzle you have a responsibility to step up and step out. Let's look at the how to of living on purpose.

If you are reading Energy 4 Life and putting the teachings into practice, you will already be half way there. That's assuming you are not already living on purpose and of course you may well be. This process will merely take you to your next level.

To really step out on purpose in life we need to resonate with natural law. We need to tune into a higher vision for our lives, as Oprah says, *"the universe is dreaming a bigger dream for you than you dream for yourself"*. This process of involution that I call Spirit of Success forms the coaching aspect of E4L. We work with natural law bringing spirit into manifestation through you. Everything you dream of, that is in alignment with your purpose, already exists in spirit. It is just for you to align yourself, open to spirit and embrace your Divine purpose.

Spirit of Success

Start by giving thanks for your life, your health, your family, all that you have achieved to date, give thanks for all no matter how small. Cultivating an **attitude of gratitude** helps build confidence. You are already successful and you have overcome many obstacles to arrive where you are today. Take time to acknowledge and appreciate yourself, give thanks for the Divine blessings you have already received in your life.

- What has the universe got in store for you? Begin to look at what is changing in your life, what are you being asked to be, do or have right now? Close your eyes and take time to **visualize** yourself in a year from now. Create an image in your mind of where you will be, who you are with, what you are doing and how you feel. How does it look to be ......? Remember *what we perceive and believe we can achieve.*

- As we have seen, self-talk plays an important role in creating our reality and ultimately our lives. So it makes sense to use words to our advantage. Create a positive

affirmation to use daily that supports your vision. This is one that I use by Dr Michael Beckwith[6]. '*The power of my pure intention activates the rich field of infinite potential.*' Another by the same author is '*Health and wholeness are my divine inheritance! I express them fully.*' You can also get specific, like, '*Right now in this moment I am open to being in the right relationship – Right now I attract abundance* and *spiritual fulfilment.*'

- I suggest sharing your goals with people. This challenges your commitment, allows people to support you either practically or by holding you accountable. Plus words create greater clarity and clarity makes your dreams reality.

- **Passion** and **motivation** are the next stages of the Spirit of Success. Passion is a major motivational force. This quality is often lacking in modern lifestyles yet we require this powerful force more today than ever. Re-connect with this energy and use it as fuel to achieve your goals. Ask yourself 'How you feel about.......?' 'What would it take to get you really excited about ....?' Get your enthusiasm up and your fire burning. Put your heart and soul into it. When your heart is in something you are more likely to plan carefully and be successful. Clarify your goals. Be aware that *a goal is a dream with a completion date.*

- When we are truly motivated **action** is the natural next step. Action is the distance between failure and success. In order to be successful we must act on our dreams, ideas and wishes. A Chinese proverb says '*Man with open mouth wait long time for roast Duck to fly in*'. We must be willing to act. 'So what are you going to do?' 'When are you going to do it?' These are questions to ask yourself. Create schedules and hire a life coach to support you and hold you accountable.

- On completion and every step of the way acknowledge your progress, praise yourself like you would a child taking its first step. Give thanks for all no matter how small. Return to an **attitude of gratitude** and the circle of life continues.

Follow the Spirit of Success process and energy will flow from the subtle realms of your vision and insight becoming manifest in your life. Goals will be achieved. Energy flows from the universe down to earth, your intentions and actions shape it. We are co-creators, shaping energy with every thought, feeling and action.

Having explored your values, released limiting beliefs and re-written your life scripts your energy will be high and flowing. You deserve to feel great. Like Sarah the nutritionist who decided to let go of negative energy and focus on her family and studies. When you change your thinking, how you feel changes which positively impacts your behaviour. Your Divine purpose can be expressed. The choice is yours – will you choose expansive free flowing energy and embrace your glorious destiny?

Chapter 7

Energy Foods - Rainbow Diet

"There is never enough food to feed a hungry Soul"
Gabriel Cousens

Eating for Energy

High energy living is reliant on high energy foods. The quality of energy in your body relates directly to what you digest in life on every level, physically, emotionally and spiritually. To risk repeating a commonly used term, *you are what you eat*. Eat a high energy balanced diet and experience a high energy balanced life. E4L explores how the food we eat affects our energy levels and wellbeing. High energy foods, rich in color, live and raw where possible have a higher vibratory frequency. A high energy diet keeps the body vibrant, healthy and free from disease. It figures that a poor diet will do the opposite, cause fatigue and ill health. We all know energy comes from the food we eat, and most people know what a healthy diet consists of. Yet many people still choose to eat unhealthily and in energy terms they drain their own resources by maintaining poor eating habits. It's not just what we eat, but when we eat, where, how and how much we eat.

Diet and nutrition is not merely about food and its raw ingredients. Why is it, nothing beats mothers or home cooking? Food is energy. The way it is grown, prepared and served. The attitude of the cook, the colors and textures, all contribute to the energy of the food and that is what nourishes. Call it energy nutrition, these aspects feed your soul.

E4L brings to light the unconscious processes behind food choice. This helps you understand the energy of food and how to make better choices. A rainbow diet of varied plant based foods vegetables, fruits, nuts eaten in their raw and live state, as nature intended, is by far the best way to eat. What differs for each one of us is when, where, how and how much we eat. For example, I don't eat breakfast. I choose mornings to fast and continue the process of elimination. Mid morning I have a juice or green juice. Some people cannot manage the day without breakfast.

You must know not only what the experts say, but also what your body says. Enjoy the ritual of honoring your body and savoring your food. Develop conscious eating habits and you will radiate high energy.

There is so much conflicting information when it comes to food, eating, weight loss, rejuvenation and general health and wellbeing. It is said that, *one man's medicine is another man's poison*. This is due to different constitutions, lifestyles, metabolic rates and personal preferences. Eating is very individual, I have had people criticizing me most of my life for the way I choose to eat. As a child I preferred eating organic food straight from our garden before it was cooked (over-cooked) but I was told to wait until it was ready! As a young person, friends would complain about my empty fridge. I don't need to eat a lot of food, my metabolism is very slow. As a vegetarian adult back in the day, we were called cranks! So now that I choose a high raw diet I am practiced in honoring my body temple and being true to myself, despite what people say. Choosing a high energy conscious diet may threaten people close to you. They may feel that it asks them to consider what they themselves eat, and if they don't want to do that it's easier to criticize you. So beware, don't try to impose your ideas on others, invite them only if they ask.

If you are changing your diet, be clear why you are doing so. Make a resolve to honour your body and your highest self. Set yourself some guidelines that support change. Then value your health and spiritual development enough to stay with what truly honors your body, mind and spirit.

Rainbow Diet

Ask yourself, *do I live to eat or eat to live*? Regardless of how you view food the important thing to remember is that we are eating for energy. One of the first things I invite people to think about in terms of diet is color. One of the simplest ways to assess the energy of your food is by color. Eating foods throughout your day that resemble a rainbow will provide a range of nutrients and micronutrients to feed your entire system. We know the chakras form a rainbow of seven energetic rays from root to crown. Simply introducing all the colors of the rainbow onto your daily menu increases the energy of your food and internal organs. The natural colors found in food provide essential nutrients and are also nature's way of harmonizing and communicating with us. Each color resonates with a specific chakra which relates to the endocrine glands and nervous system before extending energy to your entire body.

In my workshops I ask people what the main difference is between junk food and healthy food. We then look at images of both. Think about it for a moment. The main difference is color. Junk food has no natural colour, it is bleached and then artificial coloring may be added. So try to avoid the whites – flour, bread, pasta, potatoes and rice. They all come in healthier whole-food, colored versions. Another thing is labels, we may have been taught to read labels, but we can go one step further and recognize that most healthy foods don't have labels. Carrots, apples and spinach have no labels to read. So simply by introducing a broad range of fresh organic, colorful fruits and vegetables, you will immediately see an upward shift in the quantity and vibration of your energy levels.

In case you are thinking all the colors don't exist in food, I offer some suggestions in the chart below. There are more than three million plant based foods to choose from. When eating foods as nature intended, from plants rather than manufactured on a plant, there is no shortage of choice.

Food Colour Chart

Chakra	Colour	Foods
Root Muladhara	**Red**	Watermelon, strawberries, raspberries, apples, red pepper, tomatoes, radish, beetroots, red onion, guava, chilli, saffron, pomegranate.
Sacral Swadistana	**Orange**	Carrots, peppers, sweet potatoes, apricots, mango, squash, pumpkin, red lentils, cantaloupe melon, oranges, papaya, kumquats, orange beetroots..
Solar Plexus Manipura	**Yellow**	Banana, pears, lemon, pineapple, grapefruit, sweetcorn, plantain, quince, turnip, peppers, turmeric.
Heart Anahata	**Green**	All leafy green vegetables, lettuce, rocket, watercress, asparagus, broccoli, wheatgrass, peas, okra, broad beans, cabbage, chard, kiwi, courgette,(zucchini) lime, cucumber, apples, green beans, avocado, beetroot tops, herbs, green tea.

Throat Vishudha	**Blue**	Blue corn, blueberries, grapes, edible flowers, borage, blue broccoli.
Brow Ajna	**Indigo**	Blueberries, blackberries, black grapes, edible flowers.
Crown Saraswara	**Purple**	Cabbage, beetroot, purple corn, plums, cherries, figs, Aubergine (eggplant), sea vegetables, purple potato.

Eating a broad range of naturally coloured foods equals a nutritious diet rich in phytochemicals. This is an excellent way to make food your medicine. Phytochemicals found in fruits, herbs and vegetables have been used for centuries to cleanse, balance, heal and re-energise the body. Fresh foods are full of vitamins A, C and E plus antioxidants that are good for reducing the risk of cancer and slowing the aging process. These foods also contain some protein, calcium, potassium, iron and fiber to keep your body strong and healthy. By eating a rainbow diet, your heart, liver, digestion, immune system and eyes are all well nourished. Beautifully vibrant foods eaten as close to nature intended as possible, offer greater quantities of the key substances that prevent and fight disease. So why not take me up on my invite and eat something from every color of the rainbow every day. That way you are sure to live a high energy life.

Elements and Gunas

The color of our food provides energy. The quality and vibration of food also supplies energy. In the yogic tradition all living things including you and I, have a vibration, a specific quality and energetic frequency. These are known as gunas. The three gunas are Sattva, Rajas and Tamas. Sattva is a pure energetic state, rajas an active energetic state and tamas an inert energetic state.

So how does this relate to food? Let's take an apple or any fruit. Fruit is in its most sattvic state when ripe and just ready to fall from the tree, it is rajasic when not yet ripe. Fruit is often picked early so it can travel long distances and ripen at the destination. Tamasic fruit has already fallen from the tree and is left rotting. Do you get a sense of the differing energetic qualities? Sattva is pure balanced and neutral, rajas is more active and yang, tamasic is the negative, lifeless, yin state.

All living things can be categorized according to the three gunas. In humans, sattvic people live high energy, conscious lives, rajasic people live on the treadmill of life, while the tamasic types amongst us are still in bed procrastinating.

We each embrace all three gunas, but have a dominance that changes at different times on life's journey. As you are reading this book, maybe you have been a bit rajasic or too tamasic and are now seeking a more sattvic life. Sattvic living is high vibrational conscious living. Sattvic people make wise choices that prioritize spirit, health and harmony and that means where possible eating foods in their most sattvic state.

So far Energy Foods consists of eating rainbow coloured fruits and vegetables while they are in a fresh sattvic state, as close to nature intended as possible. Another important consideration along with color and gunas, when we are thinking of the energy of food, is the elements. The foods we eat resonate with different seasons and the four elements. In E4L we classify foods in relation to their elements.

Earth foods literally grow in the earth. They are roots and tubers like potatoes, carrots, parsnips, yams, cassava, beetroots etc. Water foods grow on the earth and contain lots of water. They tend to be salad vegetables and greens, such as various lettuce leaves, cucumber, squash and courgettes or zucchini. Fire foods grow a few feet above the ground, a harvest of grains and legumes. Fire foods are largely starches and proteins. Air foods grow up in the air and consist of fruits, nuts and seeds. In winter we tend to eat heavier comforting root vegetables and in the summer months we desire more cool watery foods. In general it's good to eat an abundance of air and water foods, along with smaller portions of earth and fire foods. Balance is the key.

Yogic Eating

My diet changed drastically when I was introduced to yoga 30 years ago. Living a yogic lifestyle and eating according to yogic principles has been one of the best things I have ever done. I am sure along with the melanin in my skin, my diet is responsible for me looking at least a decade younger and more on a good day. I have always enjoyed people being surprised by my age. I have amused myself by proudly saying I was born in the 1950s, I only just made it in, but it has given me lots of laughs. So what is the secret of the yoga of food?

Yoga is the art and science of creating union. It's a blending of the personal and transpersonal aspects of self. The purpose is to reach a state of oneness, bliss, ecstasy where the Creator and the created become one, the lover and beloved unite. This level of heightened consciousness requires mindfulness and inner peace. It can take lifetimes to master. A healthy body-mind facilitates the spirits journey and full expression. When the mind is agitated it is not possible to hear the still small voice within.

Foods play a major role in stimulating the activity of the mind. They can either activate or calm. The foods we eat can cause over activity and stress, leading to illness and disease. Or we can make choices that lead to health in body, mind and spirit.

Yoga teachings go beyond the actual food we eat and incorporate why, when, what, and how we eat. Eating is a very pleasurable activity. This is because it is one of the few things we can do that truly stimulates, satiates and satisfies all our senses. We can really enjoy the sensual experience of touching, smelling, tasting, seeing and hearing our food. As good as this is, it's not the reason we eat. The sensual is a bonus, we eat for energy. We eat to live. We must nourish and feed every cell in our bodies with high quality energy in order for them to function fully. Why we eat is really that simple. So let's move on and explore when, what and how.

In our busy 21st Century lives, when to eat is an issue. How many people are guilty of eating on the run? Not great for digestion. If I eat on the go, I never feel really satisfied and can overeat as a result. It's good to stop and take time to eat. Exactly when is very individual. You know your own body. However in E4L I offer some general guidelines. Eating late at night is not advisable, the digestive fire is slowing down and you do not require the energy. Avoid eating for at least four hours before you sleep and see how this resonates with you. Likewise in the morning it is not always necessary to eat a large meal. The system is slowly waking up and is not utilizing lots of energy. The morning is a time of elimination. Water with a slice of lemon should be taken on waking and a while later you can enjoy fruits whole or juiced. This facilitates cleansing, while supplying the body with natural sugars and energy without stressing your digestive system. As activity peaks during the day and more energy is required more food can be eaten. Lunch is a good time to enjoy a larger meal as there is still time to use the energy created. In the evening a lighter meal can be enjoyed before preparing to fast for the night. If you require snacks during the day choose from air and water foods. Nuts, seeds, fresh fruits, crudités made from raw carrots, cucumber and celery. Be mindful when you eat.

We have already looked at what to eat in the rainbow diet, let's deepen this by exploring quality and quantity. I am referring to the quality of energy produced. We all know that overeating drains energy, like eating takeouts, fast food and too many carbohydrates. A common ritual in the UK and the US is eating a Sunday roast or pot roast, consisting of roast beef or chicken, roast potatoes and vegetables. Copious quantities are eaten and the afternoon is then spent on the couch recovering. The senses may be satisfied but energy wise, this is daylight robbery. Eating too many earth and fire foods drains energy.

Given that our aim is to create high energy conscious lives, it's better to fast than overeat. Many people, me included, think we are hungry when in fact we are thirsty. Drinking more and eating less helps to maintain high energy levels.

Digesting food requires energy with some foods needing more energy to digest than they provide. Processed, canned, ready-made, microwaved, overcooked and junk foods are empty foods in energy terms. They provide calories but poor quality nutrition. Processed foods are often robbed of nutrition during production and synthetic nutrients are re-introduced. These are harder for your body to absorb. Empty food taxes your liver which has to filter out the toxins and is hard on the digestive system causing bloating, IBS (irritable bowel syndrome) and worse. The body literally doesn't recognize half of the things people eat and drink these days. I advised my sister recently if it doesn't grow on a tree, don't drink it; with the exception of water of course. There are so many colored drinks available. They are no more than water, sugar and coloring with the occasional bubble added. I call them all *poisons*, which is essentially what they are, synthetic and totally alien to your body and its inner chemistry. The number one health drink is H_2O.

Back to quantity, again this is very individual but in parts of the world where food is abundant, most people overeat. We need surprisingly small amounts of food to maintain our health. The better the quality of the food we eat, the less quantity is required.

This leads us onto the how to of eating.

Seven Conscious Eating Guidelines

1. Fill your stomach half with food, a quarter with water and leave a quarter empty. This allows maximum digestion and maximum energy to be gained from the food you eat.
2. Avoid eating and drinking together. Drink thirty minutes before eating and two hours after eating. This keeps digestive fire burning and leaves enzymes and digestive juices undiluted.
3. 'Drink your food' and 'eat your drink'. Meaning masticate your food thoroughly and drink liquids slowly. This is because digestion begins in the mouth.
4. Avoid eating or preparing food when you are feeling overly emotional, upset or angry in any way, as negative vibrations can affect food. Prepare and eat food in a relaxed state of mind.
5. Prepare food consciously, infusing it with positive loving energy. Pray or repeat a mantra as you work. Bless your food before eating.
6. Try eating in silence sometimes, it raises consciousness and can reduce the quantity of food required.
7. Fast[1] regularly, one day a month, or even once a week to completely rest your digestive organs. Drink only water or enjoy a mono diet, eating one fruit such as grapes or water-melon for restoring health. (Seek your doctors support before fasting)

Healing Power of Water

There is no better way to lift energy than drinking water. Fatigue, headaches, digestive problems and low energy levels are often alleviated simply by drinking more water. Yet it is estimated that as many as 75% of the population are dehydrated. Humans are

70-80% water. Water is crucial; every function of your body needs water. No other drink can replace water. Water is the universal solvent. It dissolves more substances than any other liquid and carries chemicals, nutrients and minerals around your body. It also transports oxygen and removes toxins on a cellular level.

As well as all this scientists are showing that water holds an energetic vibration, memory and information. This explains why homeopathy is so powerful when no trace of the original substance exists. Water itself holds the information. We know water has healing properties. We also know that it is recommended to drink 6-8 glasses daily. Drink the best quality water available to you. If you have a nearby mountain spring or sacred well, drink. If you have a water purifier or filter promising to turn tap water into spring water, drink. If you are buying water from the store, drink. If you have pure coconut water freshly delivered from local trees, drink. Bless your water to elevate its energy and vibration. Give thanks for the valuable gift water is to your body, mind and spirit. Like breath, water is the foundation of all life, we cannot live without this precious fluid. So if you have an abundance of drinking water available, give thanks, you are blessed.

No other drink has more benefits than water, it is the ultimate health drink. Water is the difference between a grape and a raisin. Humans start life in utero as around 90% water, children are 77-85% water, adults 65-80%, elders 50-60% and with age we can have as little as 40-50% before becoming raisin-like and finally dying. The first thing that happens if you are taken ill and hospitalized is you get put on a saline drip. Salt and water! Water is the difference between life and death. Your blood is 80% water, lungs 90% and your brain is 85%. Keeping your body hydrated is an effective, low cost remedy for many ails.

Water is a powerful anti-oxidant, reducing oxidation in the body. It also helps maintain healthy ph levels. If your body becomes too acidic and toxic due to dehydration and reduced oxygen levels, cellular damage can occur, creating disease and increasing the aging process.

Simply increasing your water intake has enormous healing power. Research at the University of Washington has shown that drinking five glasses of water daily reduces the risk of colon cancer by 35%, risk of breast cancer by 79% and bladder cancer by 50%. It seems when it comes to drinking water, it's the only place where going for gold is not recommended. A well hydrated body will pass clear not gold urine. So to avoid dehydration, always check the color of your urine and drink water until your urine is clear.

Water Cleansing

Think of water as liquid energy to nourish, heal and rejuvenate your body. During sleep your body is fasting for 8-10 hours, so on waking, before you break your fast, drink 1 to 1 ½ litres of water with lemon and a little Himalayan salt. This will totally flush out your digestive system and cleanse your body. Lots of illness is caused by putrefied food waste staying too long in the intestines. A water cleanse rids the colon of gases and toxic waste matter, as well as hydrating your body's cells and reducing toxins.

I have used this practice successfully myself and introduced it to clients and E4L Coaches, it is a great way of detoxing the system and maintaining health.

Dr Batmanghelidj, author of *"Your body's many cries for water,"* speaks of many healing benefits from headaches, back pain, degenerative diseases to cancer. He say's: *"It's no miracle just common sense"*. I couldn't agree more. When energy levels are low reach for H_2O.

High Energy Raw Food

Eating raw and live food plays an important role in the holistic treatment of serious health conditions like immune disorders and cancers. It is also becoming a popular lifestyle choice for the health conscious and eco warriors amongst us. Raw food has been called the yoga of food. It can be a very sattvic way of eating that re-energises the body, mind and spirit. Eating food as nature intended in its raw and live state calms the system and keeps the body feeling energised and light. It is the perfect choice for high energy living. Live foods are foods with seeds that can still grow and reproduce. Canned and processed foods have no life force. Alfalfa and various sprouts are perfect examples, as are fruits and vegetables.

Raw plant based foods provide an abundance of energy and enzymes which are essential to life. Enzymes are catalysts for all your body's chemical activities.

As much as 80% of our DNA code relates to enzymes. They are the life force accelerating change on a cellular level. Without these protein transformers life would not be possible.

There are three categories of enzymes:

1. Metabolic, around 3,000 which are responsible for managing your body.
2. Digestive enzymes, around 12 responsible for breaking down and digesting food.
3. Food enzymes, many thousands, found in raw food, that start food digestion.

Enzymes in food can be destroyed when heated above 118 degrees F or 47 degrees C. A good rule is not to heat your food above body temperature (98.6°F - 37°C). Digestive enzymes also decrease with age. A raw food diet consisting of organic fruits, vegetables, nuts, seeds, sprouted grains and legumes, cold pressed oils, avocado, sea vegetables, algaes, coconut water and superfoods, eaten as nature intended, preserves enzymes in food and your digestive enzymes. Destroying enzymes in food causes the enzymes in your body to work harder and get depleted quicker. Cooking foods denatures them. It changes the molecular structure, reduces water content, diminishes available vitamins and minerals and often totally destroys the enzymes. When the enzymes are lowered in food your body works harder to digest and absorb nutrients. Hence after eating a cooked meal your body may feel heavy and your energy levels low.

Raw food eating is not new, it is our original diet. Our earliest ancestors roamed the earth eating fruits, nuts and berries, long before they discovered fire and tools for killing animals, and well before the development of agriculture. Most of our existence as humans has been spent on a high energy raw diet. The 1960s saw an increase in all things natural and the vegan raw food diet was developed as a holistic treatment. Today more and more people are adopting this style of eating for health and ecological reasons.

I was introduced to raw eating in the 1980s by Leslie Kenton, the health and beauty expert and author of numerous books on eating raw foods for energy and wellbeing. I experienced the benefits immediately. Eating raw resonates with me, I rarely cooked anyway and have been accused of thinking a smoothie is a meal. So the fashionable new wave of raw has seen me adopt and recommend a high raw diet. 100% raw food is recommended for healing and regenerating the body. It is also ideal for weight loss programmes. As raw is the yoga of food eating, 100% raw is great for spiritual elevation, it can be used as a support along with other spiritual practices to raise energy levels and lift your spirit.

Raw food advocates eat anything from 50-100% raw. I choose an 80% high raw, high energy diet. The remaining 20% of my diet may be steamed, grilled or baked, as some starches need cooking to liberate energy. Try to avoid boiling and frying food.

I recommend finding a diet that works for you. Unless you are ill it's not necessary to be too extreme. Lots of raw foodists, live on raw chocolate and superfoods. Not so healthy. Simply changing the proportions of your food can have huge benefits. If you usually eat 80% cooked food and 20% raw, having salad and fruit with your meals, think about making the salad larger and the cooked food smaller. Start there and slowly build up as you learn how to prepare more than salad and smoothies. There is a learning curve needed to transition to the raw way of life. Balance is crucial. As your energy levels rise and your health improves you will gradually and naturally increase you raw food intake.

21 Reasons for Adopting a High Energy Raw Food Lifestyle

1. More than 3 million plant foods to choose from
2. More live you eat – more alive you will feel
3. Feel lighter, more alert, clear minded, enjoy higher energy levels
4. Raise your energetic vibration and elevate consciousness
5. Eliminate number one health issue – lack of energy
6. High nutrition foods – preserves vitamins, minerals, enzymes and phytochemicals
7. Increase water intake by eating fresh foods
8. Eat as many avocados and mangoes as you like
9. Really taste your food for the first time
10. Masticate food longer – therefore release more enzymes and improve digestion; use enzymes from your food and preserve enzymes from your body
11. Alkalises your body – needed for healing and maintaining health
12. Increases elimination, cleanses and detoxifies your system
13. Less stress on digestion, liver, intestines etc.
14. Reduces stress on your entire body
15. Controls optimum weight
16. You'll reverse signs of ageing – 80 year olds can have the

energy and look of 50 year olds. 50 year olds look 30.

17. Extends the length and quality of your life
18. You are in control of what you eat, you can source and grow your own organic food
19. Vegan raw organic diet is a responsible choice as it feeds more of the world's population and is kinder to animals and the eco system.
20. Much less expensive to eat good food than to pay for medical treatment
21. You will be an inspiration to others

Food as Medicine – 7 Superfoods for Health and Healing

1. **Earth:** we have the same makeup as our earth, so it is an excellent healer. Clay gently attracts, absorbs and neutralizes poisons both on and in the body, especially from the intestines.

2. **Water:** we are 70-80% percent water, it is our finest medicine.

3. **Lemon:** is a valuable all round cleanser, it aids digestion, alkalizes the body, purifies the blood, stimulates and decongests the liver. It is also a remedy for coughs, colds and respiratory problems.

4. **Garlic:** is anti- everything! A powerful antiseptic and disinfectant. A natural way to kill bacteria and protect against illness. It's great for rheumatic conditions. Plus an excellent appetite stimulant and digestive aid. Must be taken raw to preserve active medicinal properties.

5. **Spirulina:** Should be part of any vegetarian diet. A freshwater plant that has more protein than soy, more Vitamin A than carrots and more iron than beef. It also has B12[2] and is a rich

source of phytochemicals including GLA. Spirulina cleanses feeds and protects the body.

6. **Wheatgrass Juice:** a powerful medicine with a chemical make-up similar to our blood. Research shows it fights tumours without creating toxicity, reduces acidity, cleanses the blood, lowers high blood pressure, boosts the immune system, increases red blood cells and inhibits cell-destroying agents. It is the number one choice of alternative treatment for immune disorders and cancers.

7. **Sprouts:** Sprouts are freshly germinated, easily digested seeds and pulses. They are live plants rich in life force energy, enzymes, antioxidants, essential nutrients and chlorophyll – liquid sunshine. Sprouts restore health, slow aging and strengthen your entire body. A variety of sprouts are staples of the raw food diet.

Fasting: I have spoken a lot about eating, however where energy is concerned, fasting is also very beneficial. Abstaining from food for one day a week while consuming copious amounts of water, is good for body, mind and spirit. It rests the digestive system, releases energy, calms the mind and elevates the spirit. I highly recommend it.

Make sure you always include the above seven medicinal foods in your diet. They have shown themselves over thousands of years to aid digestion, purify the internal organs and heal the body. They are vital to the restoration and maintenance of health.

Digestion

You will see from all the above that one of the main benefits of a raw diet is the increase in enzymes and digestive function. We eat for energy, so the more efficient your digestion is the more energy you will have. And of course a poor sluggish digestion results in low energy levels. Digestive problems are the root of many ails, from headaches and skin conditions, tiredness and memory loss to weight problems, IBS and exhaustion.

We should avoid food waste getting held up in the intestines. This happens for three reasons.

1. Overeating,
2. Eating the wrong foods
3. Drinking insufficient water

Many people feel when they empty their bowels they are releasing waste from a recent meal. For example eat a big meal Monday night, pass the waste from it on Tuesday morning. No! Food transit times vary considerably according to what you eat. Humans have a long intestine; carnivores have a short intestine which allows waste to move through quickly. When we eat meat and heavy starches particularly in excess with insufficient water, waste from food eaten Monday may not be released until Friday, four days later. Even longer in some cases. If you eat three big meals a day you should evacuate three times a day, two meals twice a day, one main meal once a day will suffice. If you don't evacuate daily you are constipated. If you eat three meals and evacuate once, you create a backlog of waste matter in the intestines and end up feeling heavy and very bloated.

The problem with waste matter staying in the intestines too long especially animal waste is it continues to decay and putrefy in your body. The longer it stays the more foul it becomes creating strong smells and gaseousness. And that is not all. The real problem is your colon which is responsible for absorbing water and some vitamins, as well as forming and eliminating faeces. The longer faeces stay in your colon the more water is absorbed, making them hard and difficult to pass. The water from them is re-circulated through your body. This can create illness.

Rapid transit time is 12-36 hours. This is great for health and energy levels and can be achieved with a high raw diet. The average is 65- 100 hours. The less time dietary toxins are in contact with your colon the less time they have to be absorbed into your bloodstream. If you suffer from digestive problems or any of the ailments mentioned earlier, you may need to monitor your digestion, check transit times and consider a detoxification programme. You could begin with the water cleanse. Check transit times by eating lots of sesame seeds and waiting for them to be passed, or beetroot and observing color changes.

You can greatly improve your digestion by changing to a high raw rainbow diet. This will ensure rapid transit times, higher enzyme content, better nutrition and better health. As your consciousness raises around food choice and you understand the gunas and embrace the yoga of food – the what, when, and how, you will see tremendous shifts in your health. Remember, nothing tastes as good as being healthy feels.

Your body will be lighter, you'll look younger and your weight will regulate assuming your ideal weight. Health issues both mild and severe improve, if not dissolve completely. Energy levels certainly improve. Your cells will be fed and rejuvenated from the inside out. Your mind will be clearer and spirit lifted. Adopt Energy Foods and you will feel re-energized in body, mind and spirit. Never forget we eat for energy and no amount of food can feed a hungry soul.

Chapter 8

Energy Balance – Relaxation and Meditation

"How beautiful it is to do nothing and then rest afterwards."
Renee Locks

Energy Debt

Food is not alone in its need for digestion. In energy terms all events, experiences, encounters and emotions in life need to be digested and absorbed. This is easy with life's pleasures, the memorable fun times absorb easily. However, some things can make us sick, others get on our nerves, we get tired and energetically injured by incidents throughout life. The traumatic and painful experiences literally need to be eliminated. Yet it can be difficult to eliminate some experiences and the resulting emotions. Sometimes we chew things over, trying to find ways to assimilate them. Undigested emotions threaten stability and throw the body, mind, spirit, continuum off balance.

We also get caught up in the fast lane of life. From the moment we wake to the moment we sleep its non-stop action. If we do stop it's often only to partake in a stimulant such as coffee, tea and other caffeinated drinks. Or smoke cigarettes and eat chocolate, which also, contrary to popular opinion, stimulates the body. If we are not stimulating and overworking the system we are draining it through overwork, exhaustion, constant worrying, and not allowing enough time to re-fuel. These days many people have what I call energy debt, they are running on empty! Think about it, even your car gets an MOT and regular service. No one expects a vehicle to run on empty and I am sure you always give your car the best fuel you can afford.

So how about you, where is the balance? After all, most of us do want increased vitality, better relationships and high-energy living. Undigested emotions, running on empty and personal energy crisis are common side effects of 21st Century living. There is little consideration of stress and where it leads.

Modern living is largely devoid of spiritual rituals and habits that build energy and raise consciousness. E4L is all about regaining conscious awareness and reclaiming health, happiness and success. Slowing down the pace of life and living consciously can mean the difference between life and death. It's imperative to maintain the flow of energy throughout your body, mind and spirit this is the secret of balanced health. In order to do this we need ways of re-balancing our energy such as alignment techniques and tools that instantly affect the nervous system inducing rest, deep relaxation and meditation. This reduces your bodies stress chemicals, balances emotions and promotes energy flow

It's all about creating ease within, because when you are not creating ease in your life you are creating dis-ease. It's said that *life is a gift with no receipt, no guarantee, and no user manual, you didn't pay for it, and it's your responsibility to make it work.*

If you want your life to work on many levels Energy Balance is the key.

Energy Balance

Our bodies are very finely tuned and have an amazing ability to self-regulate. A feedback mechanism interfaces with the environment and relays messages to the brain. If our temperature changes as little as 1° C up or down the body will automatically sweat or shiver to maintain optimum balance. The liver filters out potentially dangerous toxins, like alcohol, metals, and other poisons. It also makes sure we don't run out of vital substances like Vitamin A, D and B12. Our kidneys carefully balance water and salt levels in the body. Hormone release is monitored so all activities function optimally. The body is an incredible feat of engineering, carefully created and balanced for function and pleasure. Yet we seldom honour this sacred masterpiece; failing to recognise that we are *the* ultimate creation that has taken 14 billion years to come into being.

Humans are the pinnacle of evolution in our universe. All life is a sacred evolutionary journey, a process of continuous unfolding and becoming. This journey of energy, information and consciousness continues to breathe through us, unfolding what I refer to as the Ongoing Evolutionary Process (OEP). The OEP is expressing through, around, and as you in this moment. It is your inner power, the still small voice, a passion, a knowing. We have a response-ability to recognise and honour the evolution of life in all its vastness and all its richness. You can tap into the OEP and listen to its unfolding whenever there is stillness, silence and mindfulness.

When we create space for balance we allow the system to self-regulate on a deep energetic level. Long held pain or emotional debris can be digested and eliminated without cognitive awareness. In most cases when we work with energy and the body we bypass the need for analysis and understanding. Energy Balance can rest, refuel and heal the body more in half an hour than a full night's sleep. Sleep is often fraught with physical tension and worries. Energy Balance allows the greater intelligence that moves through you to rejuvenate your entire system. It also allows you to connect with the OEP developing inner knowledge and a greater desire for and awareness of purpose, passion and peace.

Energy Balance uses tools like breath awareness, relaxation, meditation, alignment techniques and hands on bodywork. Inner stability is re-established as the body, mind, spirit is fully integrated. We aim to expand the breath, slow the heart rate, focus the mind, induce stillness and increase presence in the body, mind, spirit.

It's about getting out of the head and into the body in order to facilitate the journey of the soul. Energy Balance brings about greater connection to the Divine intelligence that moves through you.

Relaxation in E4L is a not a dreamlike state lacking in awareness, more so it is relaxed yet attentive and mindful. During relaxation the PSNS (internal brakes) is activated and the right brain is utilized. The body can self-regulate and re-energize. We also tune to a higher vibratory frequency where we can generate and accumulate energy. The right brain given this opportunity often offers solutions to problems instantly. Clearing the mind through deep relaxation releases stagnation and orders fragmented thoughts. When energy is not flowing freely we can get very scattered, with poor concentration and a busy mind. In this situation relaxation eludes us. Energy Balance restores harmony and integration allowing the whole brain to work efficiently and free us from limited and hectic patterns. As energy shifts and perspectives change, we become less rigid and more open to spirit. Life's many experiences start to be seen as lessons on a journey of living, loving and learning.

When energy is balanced and expansive we are less reliant on external things and other people for peace and happiness. Instead we know peace and happiness are choices we can make for ourselves. Negatives fall away and we become thankful for the challenges and opportunities they bring. We learn to tap into the OEP and connect with the infinite power within.

Anatomy of Stress

Your body's ability to self-regulate and maintain internal balance is largely controlled by the Autonomic Nervous System, which is divided into two parts.

1. The Sympathetic Nervous System SNS – your accelerator
2. The Parasympathetic Nervous System PSNS – your brakes

The SNS activates your body it's the accelerator that gets you moving in the morning. Chemicals flood into your pituitary gland triggering your adrenals setting up a whole wave of activities. Your body's primitive reaction to perceived threat is known as the flight or fight response. It's also sometimes called the 'startle response'.

For example: Let's say your alarm clock goes off. Your SNS is stimulated and releases chemicals into your body for acceleration. Your body thinks an emergency is taking place and wants you to have enough energy to cope with it. In fact, you are not doing anything just getting up. You get ready for work, have a quick breakfast and jump in your car. While in your car you find yourself in a traffic jam and start getting irritated, more chemicals are released and you're still not really doing anything, just sitting in your car. You are now late for work and your office rings on your mobile phone, infuriating you and giving rise to more chemicals. You finally get to work and find out there has been a major problem since you left yesterday, more chemicals are added to the cocktail. It's still only nine o'clock in the morning and you have triggered enough chemicals to fight a sabre toothed tiger or run a marathon. And what do you do sit down and drink coffee, which further stimulates your SNS and even more excess chemicals flood the system.

We do this and worse day after day; flooding the system with adrenalin, stimulants and startle wastes. It is this insistence on constant acceleration, foot on the SNS that leads to stress related dis-orders. The body basically doesn't get enough time to clean up. It is stressed!

The PSNS, which I think of as your internal brake, balances your nervous system. It regulates and neutralises excess chemicals. I see it as a cleansing system. It calms and relaxes having an opposite effect to the SNS. But we simply don't activate it enough. In fact it may feel quite uncomfortable when the body starts to slow down and relax. This discomfort finds people reaching for cigarettes, coffee, coke and other stimulants to trigger the more familiar feeling of acceleration.

Do you see what happens? You can actually get addicted to stress chemicals and startle wastes. The minute your body starts to clean up, it can feel so unfamiliar that you immediately reach for some form of stimulation. Then you feel relaxed. And fool yourself into believing that cigarettes chocolate and coffee are relaxing and good for you.

The five worst things you can do when you feel stressed:

1. Take more stimulants coffee, chocolate and cigarettes
2. Ignore your body's signals, tension, tightness, fatigue
3. Self medicate with alcohol and drugs
4. Judge your stress levels by those of other people
5. See stress as your enemy

Stress is your body's way of calling you to attention and greater consciousness. Stimulants like coffee, chocolate, cigarettes prevent your PSNS, your brakes from cleaning your body effectively. Thus continuing the startle response and causing all manner of stress related symptoms. If you feel the need for more coffee, carbohydrates or sweet things know that it's time to put the brake on.

Knots, tension in your stomach, tightness in your shoulders, fatigue in your eyes, or your concentration flagging are signs not to run for coffee but to put the brakes on and relax. If sleeping is difficult and you find yourself self-medicating with alcohol or other drugs it's time to put the brakes on. If your back aches and your energy is low put the brake on. When you have been talking non-stop all day to colleagues, friends, children and now yourself, brake! Think Energy Balance.

When your internal dialogue turns negative, fearful and you are constantly irritable and worried, it's a sign that you need to rest. If you are getting over emotional, angry, tearful, loud, violent, please put the brakes on. If you are procrastinating and avoiding the obvious or if you are tired and anxious, stressed out by doing too much, it is time to stop and put the brake on.

Stress is not our enemy. It is an important part of life. But if we continually build up startle chemicals in our systems and never relax long enough to remove them, then we have a problem. That's why Energy Balance is so important. Energy Balance seeks equal amounts of energy coming in as energy going out.

Research suggests that women respond to stress differently from men and rather than a flight of fight response, women are prone to tend and befriend. We want to share our thoughts and feelings, joining together and supporting each other in times of stress. We have seen an increase in pamper parties and spa days used to release stress. Research indicates this it is exactly what women need to do! I offer the E4L programme as a retreat for this reason. We must learn to ease up on acceleration, put the brakes on and stop regularly to rest and relax, so we can energize and re-balance the body, mind, spirit continuum.

Energy Balance invites rest and relaxation into your life and as a result you will experience a biochemical and energetic shift. You will find your mind calmer, blood pressure lower, breathing slower, pulse rate relaxed and your digestion will improve. Plus, you will sleep better. These are tried and tested physiological benefits of stimulating your PSNS and allowing your body and mind to relax. These are measurable results. You will also enjoy more energy, mental clarity and a sense of renewed well-being.

Energy Anatomy

There are different maps of the energy body in different cultures. The two main ones are the acupuncture meridian system developed in China and the chakra system developed in India. Knowledge of energy anatomy goes back to the very beginning of time, when the first humans walked on the sacred land we call Africa. They lived at the mercy of the elements and understood the relationship between their surroundings of earth, water, fire/sun, air and the elements that dwelt within. They gave us the first energy anatomy, known as the four or five element system.

Earth: relates to the physical, it is the densest element, the crystallisation of spirit into matter. **Water:** flows, soothes, nourishes and cleanses, it promotes fertility, creativity and emotion. Water is a great healer and sacred friend. **Fire:** is the great transformer full of vitality, warmth and excitement. It both destroys and creates. It's an often abused and feared element. **Air:** is more subtle and light with a quality of freedom and change. It is the sacred giver of life. The fifth element known as **Ether** is the primordial space from which all else arises.

The elements are found today in almost every culture's spiritual, philosophical, healing and mythological traditions. I explore this in my first book, *Opening to Spirit,* detailing extensively the characteristics of each element and the migration of spiritual tradition from a common beginning in Africa. This Ancient and rich legacy remains valuable today acting as an organising principle that helps us manage and utilise a vast array of personal experience.

Working with thousands of people worldwide over 25 years, both in sickness and in health, has helped me understand that it is not the energy map that is important. The maps differ significantly, yet all systems based on energy are very effective. My interest and question has always been 'what is it that actually works?' In E4L we recognize that the map is not the territory, therefore we don't spend a lot of time learning Ancient energy maps. Instead we focus solely on the movement of energy. We recognise that any manifestation of illness, psychological issues, lack of spiritual direction, questions about the meaning and purpose of life, are all caused by a disturbance in the flow of energy. One cause requires one solution and that solution is to restore balanced, free flowing energy to the body, mind, spirit continuum. When energy flows freely from the universal source to your core centre, health, happiness, success and fulfilment can be maintained, re-established or created depending on which is necessary.

We don't use a specific map but we do work with the chakras and the elements, which have already been discussed. Plus we have an awareness of the directional flow of energy and the aura and the koshas, which are subtle sheaths of the energy anatomy. These are tools for communication allowing us to grasp a greater sense of our vastness and simplify the complexity of our humanness. I detail the directional flow, the aura and koshas below.

DIRECTIONAL FLOW OF ENERGY

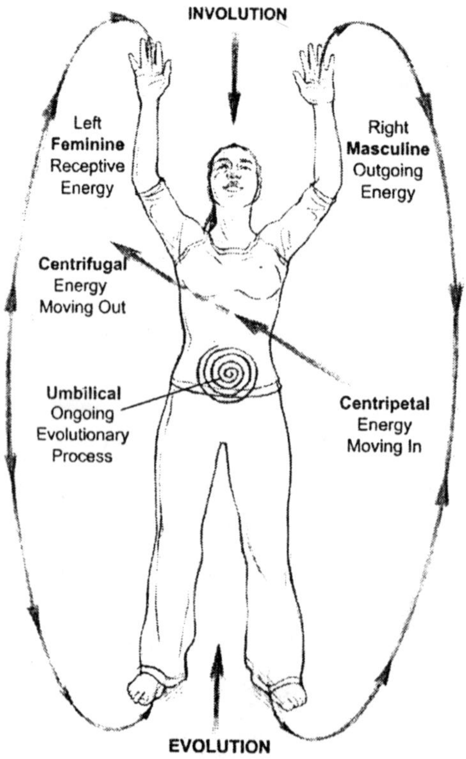

We are energy beings and energy flows in seven main directional lines of force. Spiraling through, around and manifesting as us.

Up and Down: This is the directional force of **involution** and **evolution,** the descending and ascending movement of energy. Ancient teachings tell us that energy flows from pure undifferentiated spirit to become dual then triple and continues to flow into the many. This is the process of stepping down (involving) from heaven – universe - sky to the physical earthly realm. Energy then returns (evolves) from the gross physical to the subtle and spiritual. In the body, energy flows from the head downwards and from the feet up.

In and Out: This is the **centripetal** and **centrifugal** directional force, energy moving towards and away from the centre respectively. These physics terms explain the movement of energy as it flows towards and away from you. The centripetal energy moves from the periphery into your centre. It is energy drawn in from the world and from people as we open our arms to receive energy. The centrifugal force is energy flowing away from your centre, powered by big muscles in the back of your body. This energy moves out towards other people and the world.

Left and Right: The right side of your body represents the **masculine** outgoing force of energy, it has a positive charge. While the left represents the **feminine** receptive energy with a negative charge. Energy flows out through your right arm and hand. It flows in through your left arm and hand. When the hands are placed together they create a peaceful neutral position hence its use in prayer. During the *hand energy sensing* exercise in chapter one, the positive and negative energies of the hands are often experienced and described as a magnet.

Centre: Core energy resides at the centre of your being. This is the invisible, **umbilical** energy that links you to the source of all creation. It is where we tap into the OEP - ongoing evolutionary process. It is the sacred inner power the hub at the centre of an ever evolving and spiralling wheel of power filled energy.

For optimum functioning of the HES - human energy system, and the body, mind, spirit it is essential to balance the flow of energy. While breathing we always inhale as well as exhale. To exhale only would quickly lead to expiration. The day willingly recedes into night, resting before rising again with the light. The moon stays in darkness for three nights knowing she will return again to her fullness. The universe respects the rhythm of life.

Energy Balance is an opportunity for you to rest, relax and re-energize. Balanced energy must flow in as well as out. It's not enough to drain resources and not stop to refuel. Over reliance on the worldly leads to suffering and spiritual emptiness, as energy changes and that which you felt was in the grasp of your hand vanishes, be it money, career, material possessions or people, they all change. Get out of energy debt by aiming to draw in more energy than goes out. Restore energy flow and build a reserve that can be used to create health, happiness and success.

The Aura

Subtle, auric vibrations are phenomena we are all familiar with. We speak of liking and disliking a person's vibration or vibe. This is the felt sense of energy we get when meeting people. We literally step into their aura and feel the energy. The aura is also evident when we speak with people. We don't get close to a person's face and speak into it; instead we leave a comfortable distance around the person. Some people we feel closer to than others. We step comfortably into their aura feeling safe.

We hold an unconscious awareness that people extend beyond the physical body. Part of non-verbal communication is sensing a person's aura, feeling the vibration and judging how to relate. We all sense the right moment to approach a loved one for a favour and know when to stay away. They don't have to say anything we sense the changes in their aura.

All experiences have an impact on your aura. Distress can cause energy to withdraw. Happiness does the opposite, increasing your energy field leaving you feeling open and expansive. Openness draws positive energy and people into your aura as you resonate with all the joy and happiness around you. Likewise if our energy is negative then we resonate with the negative vibes around us drawing it close. Everything we do and everyone we encounter has an impact on the aura. Positive thinking elevates and negative thinking depresses.

Unconsciously we know the aura needs adequate space for us to be healthy and happy. The aura can become restricted in places where the energetic frequency is low and draining. Likewise the aura expands in beautiful natural surroundings like the ocean or sacred mountains. Spiritual environments, places of worship, ley lines[1] on the earth, all help us extend our aura. We all have favourite places where we go to re-balance and experience some peace, even if it's simply a walk in the park. We are attracted by the potential of expanding our energy field.

Aura Awareness

If you haven't tried it yet, develop your understanding of the aura by practicing Energy Field Awareness. For the next few days pay attention to your own vibrations and the energy fields of those around you. This is explained in chapter one. Make notes in your journal on your experiences with observing energy and the aura.

Often after I have given a talk, people embrace me and comment on their surprise at how small I am. While on stage my energy field is expansive, I am reaching out and connecting with each person in the audience. Although not touching them physically, they still feel my aura and sense me to be much bigger energetically than I am physically.

During bodywork sessions I may lay my hand on someone's abdomen, connecting with their energy. When I lift my hand and move away people are surprised, as they still feel my hand touching them. What they actually experience, as a result of the session, is their own aura and expanded energy field.

Koshas

In the yogic teachings, Koshas are subtle energetic sheaths. They form an evolutionary sequence on the journey of awareness and unfolding. They transport us from the gross physical realm to the elevated state of Ananda, which is bliss. This is oneness, total absorption in the Divine. The subtle sheaths help us understand where energy is focussed at any given time. However to attain bliss we must balance each level and transcend it. We are not the physical or our thoughts, emotions etc. The word Maya used at each level, means illusion. We are pure spirit, therefore we must avoid getting caught up at any level and elevate our awareness, energy and consciousness to a state of pure undifferentiated spirit.

The Five Koshas

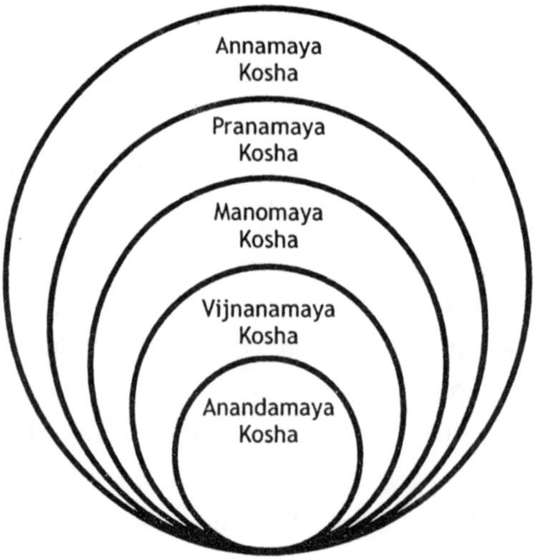

Annamaya Kosha: This is the densest sheath, the physical body and realm we are most familiar with. You have heard the expression, you are what you eat, well in Sanskrit this level is literally known as Anna-maya, anna means food. A lot of energy can be drained here through poor diet, comfort eating, sedentary lifestyles and stress. This often means our attention can be adsorbed at the level of Annamaya Kosha. A life consumed by eating, sleeping and looking for more food. Energy Foods and Energy Exercises both work to create balance on this level.

Pranamaya Kosha: This is the subtle energy body, the vital sheath and life force. In E4L we work to balance and elevate this level as it is a template and infuses all the other levels. Breathing exercises are used to purify and build energy reserves. With practice and awareness you can learn to really sense and tap into this powerful energy sheath, the body's intelligent life force.

Manamaya Kosha: The mental sheath is the realm of our thoughts, emotions, instincts and unconscious mind. This level is experienced through our senses. Energy shows itself at this level as a constant array of fluctuating, desires, passions and feelings. We often react to these energies and can feel ourselves being pulled by ego, directed by sensations of pleasure or pain and held hostage by our fears. The mind becomes attached, addicted and struggles to develop discernment and wisdom. Resting the mind through meditation helps you reach a place of greater balance.

Vijnanamaya Kosha: This is the realm of reason and intellect, it's our reflective intelligence and ability to think and create meaning. It's broader than the usual use of the word intellect as it includes wisdom, knowledge and genetic memory; the innate wisdom of seven generations past. Ego also operates at this level, creating a unique identity and sense of I am woman, man, young, old, therefore I am....., the story continues. None of it real, it is merely a picture on a movie screen. When the film ends everything ends.

Anandamaya Kosha: The bliss sheath alone is real, the causal realm. Pure energy, that gives rise to everything. This is the silent centre and witness, the eternal truth constantly unfolding, becoming and being all that you are. It's the hub at the centre of your existence that stays still as everything changes. It is Satchitanada, existence, knowledge and bliss. We have all touched this Divine existence and long for its return in our lives.

It is this drive that has you reading this book, seeking increased balance and fulfilment in your live. This deep calling to be healthy and whole, full of energy, on purpose and connected to the Great Spirit that moves within us.

The practices offered in Energy Balance bring about change on all levels of the energy anatomy. I have explained energy anatomy in some detail, however, all the tools in E4L can be successfully utilised with no knowledge of energy anatomy whatsoever. This is because all that is truly important is the rhythm found throughout our universe. This simple rhythm is the constant expansion and contraction of energy. Let's explore some tools for Energy Balance.

Hands On Bodywork

A big part of Energy Balance is hands on bodywork conducted by qualified Energy 4 Life practitioners. It provides an opportunity for the client to do nothing at all. The practitioner will ask the client to lie fully clothed on a couch, there is nothing they need to do, just relax and allow the energy to flow. The alignment, release techniques and Chakra balancing are usually carried out in silence. They are gentle techniques, consisting mainly of laying the hands in specific places to facilitate the flow of energy. Gentle rocking may be introduced and the clients own rhythm of breathing is encouraged. Deep relaxation generally results. This takes between 30-45 minutes.

Energy Balance also has practices you can carry out yourself. I introduce some of them below and invite you to incorporate them into your daily power half hour, which is your time for resting re-fuelling and re-tuning your system.

Self Help Tools

Conscious Breathing

Never underestimate the power of taking time to breathe consciously. This practice alone can totally elevate your energy levels and transform your life from stressed to blessed. Breath carries within it the animating life force. As you breathe more fully you recharge your body, calm your mind and re-balance your vital energy.

Sit comfortably with your spine upright and your legs crossed in a meditation pose or feet flat on the floor if you are on a chair. Place your palms facing up on your knees. Draw your chin slightly towards your chest in order to lengthen the back of your neck. Gently close your eyes and relax your mouth. Take up as much space in your body as you can, letting go of any tightness or tension. Release and relax your whole body. Bring attention to your breath. Place one hand over your lower abdomen.

1st part — Breathe in **slowly and fully** through your nose, raising your abdomen. Open your chest and completely fill your lungs (your hand should lift upwards).

2nd part — Hold your breath comfortably, keeping your body totally still for a count of four. (This can be increased with practice)

3rd part	Exhale slowly through your nose and empty your lungs completely. Feel your abdomen pulling down towards the floor (your hand will be lowered).

Repeat this three-part breath three to seven times.

Feel the immediate shift in consciousness. Let yourself rest allowing energy to flow freely and your consciousness to rise touching the very core of your being and blessing you with love and insight.

Relaxation – Two Minute Vacation

A simple invitation to stop whatever you are doing for a couple of minutes to slow down, relax and focus on your breath for two minutes: this will re-oxygenate your system and rebalance your energy, creating calm and greater clarity. I recommend doing this once in every hour. Give it a try!

Meditation

This ancient technique probably goes back to the beginning of civilisation, when people had time to gaze up at the stars and simply *Be*. Meditation is used for resting the continuous activity of the mind. In its pure form it can be difficult to master. For this reason many variations of meditation have been developed. You can meditate to soft relaxing music; you can use visualisation techniques or use the more traditional method of focusing on the breath and stilling the mind. The latter takes repeated practice and discipline, while you can benefit from the former almost instantly. Meditation can be utilised by everyone, everywhere to enrich the quality of life. I have seen lives completely transformed through meditation.

Chakra Meditation

This light meditation brings illumination, vision and insight. You are pure vibrational energy. Allow 35 minutes, 5 minutes on each centre.

Sit upright, close your eyes and allow yourself to enter a meditative state....Breathe easily and relax your whole being.

- Take your attention to your Root chakra focus on the colour red.......let the red ray fill your being.......
- Raise your attention to the Sacral chakra and focus on the colour orange.......let the vibration of the orange ray fill your being........
- Raise your attention to the Solar Plexus chakra, focus on the colour yellow.......let the yellow ray permeate your entire being........
- Lift your energy to the Heart chakra, home of the colours green and rose pink.......feel the colours spreading throughout your body......
- Now on to the Throat chakra, focus on the colour blue.......allow the blue ray to flow into your whole being.....
- Elevate energy to your Brow chakra see all the colours of the rainbow merge before your eyes. Allow the colours to flood your entire being....
- Ascend to your Crown chakra, the thousand petaled lotus and golden ray. Tune into the golden, shimmering light that emerges from the top of your head. Let energy stream down, like liquid gold. Covering you in powerful all embracing energy. Fill your being until it overflows, hear the whispers of wisdom. Open to spirit knowing that all is well.

Crown Chakra Meditation

The Crown chakra is the home of undifferentiated pure spirit. Meditation on pure spirit brings unity and liberation. This meditation can take 15-30 minutes.

- Sit before a candle and stare into its shining flame. Know that nothing separates you from the candle light all is made from pure vibrating energy. You are pure vibrational energy.

- Gently close your eyes, lengthen your spine and relax into the sacred space inside your Self, the place where all is still and silent. This place is deep inside, it's the very core of your being. The still central hub of the spinning chakras. This central core runs from the base chakra to the crown. It connects earth to heaven. It connects you with your Creator.

- As you enter this space everything as you know it ceases. There is only pure undifferentiated energy having no shape or form. There is nothing to fear, we originate from this very place. We know it well. But choose to forget.

- Let your spirit be re-united with the universal energy. Let your Self plunge into nothingness, reach beyond the stars and dwell in peace.

Be still and know that you are a part of the infinite vastness of the Divine Ocean.

Putting Energy Balance into Practice

The only way to achieve real benefit from Energy Balance is to practice. Make a commitment to yourself to do a little something towards balancing your energy every day. Love yourself enough to put time aside for you. Make appointments with yourself in your diary and honour yourself like you would a treasured friend. Book an appointment with an Energy 4 Life Coach to support you. If there are not any in your area, train to become one, so you can change your life and support others to change theirs.

Energy Balance Practices

Conscious Breathing
Ocean Breath
Six Pointed Star
Deviasana
Energy4Life Chakra Balance
Chakra Meditation
Two-Minute Vacation
Crown Chakra Meditation

Energy Balance offers practical tools for creating ease in your life, all you have to do is implement them regularly. The good news is it gets easy once you have experienced the results. Given the right conditions your body self-regulates, living in energy debt becomes a thing of the past, as your autonomic nervous system finds balance. Biochemical and energetic shifts take place as the energy of your Chakras re-aligns. The elements are more fully expressed as a harmonious flow of energy is restored. Your energy field and aura become alive and radiant. You will enjoy an abundance of energy and people will comment on how beautiful and vibrant you look as they sense this positive energy.

Simply investing 2, 30 or 60 minutes a day on balancing your energy will give you an infinite return. It is life assurance, a tried and tested way of releasing stress, eliminating illness, elevating your vibration and connecting with the ongoing evolutionary process unfolding within. Energy Balance deepens your connection to spirit and allows you to inherit a life of health, happiness, success and fulfilment.

Chapter Nine

Energy 4 Life Coaching

"The Doctor of the Future will give no medicine but will interest his patients in the care of the human frame, in diet and in the cause and prevention of disease"

Thomas Edison

Committing to Change

At the beginning of this book I asked you three questions.

- Would you like more **Energy and vitality?**
- Do you want to raise your **Consciousness and quality of life?**
- Are you ready for **Change**?

You have almost completed reading Energy 4 Life, this is the last chapter. So what now? One of the things I have identified with numerous clients and students, is that before they come to me they have already read lots of books and they know the theory, many could and some have, written books themselves. They come to me because the real challenge is taking action and doing things differently.

I know myself, as much as I understand the psychology of change as my area of expertise, I don't always find change easy. But once I commit that's it! It's all about commitment, who and what are you really committed to?

The previous chapters share what you need to know to live a high energy conscious life. Now all you need is to take action. So this is the most important chapter, because this is where you commit to the change you say you are ready for.

Coaching is all about getting from where you are now to where you want to be. This suggests it's useful to know where you are and also where you want to be. And of course: when you want to be there. If there is no hurry, you don't need a Coach; you will get there.......eventually. But if you would like to arrive in the foreseeable future then working with a Coach is a great idea. So for now let me be your Coach.

We all have dreams and fantasies about being healthier, happier, richer and more successful. What are you willing to do about it? The only difference between a dream and a goal is that one has commitment, a completion date and a plan to be followed by action. So this chapter is where you get clear about where you are, where you want to be and what you are really committed to changing to create your desired transformation.

Transforming the Way you Live

Let's look at where a lot of people are these days and then explore where you are personally. I have had the privilege of working with thousands of people all over the world. From my experience I have observed five main ways people allow their personal energy resources to get drained.

1. **Overwork** is the number one energy zapper. The culture of working long hours in the office or working from home without clear boundaries causes tiredness, poor concentration and eventually leads to exhaustion.
2. **Reluctance to exercise** takes the number two spot. We all know the benefits of exercise yet travelling by car and sitting down all day creates insufficient movement, which is a major energy zapper and cause of stress.
3. **Poor diet** is another issue, people eat foods lacking in vitality and nutritional value. Eating on the move and yo-yo dieting prevent nutrients being adequately absorbed. We need to consume foods that provide energy and

sustain life. Most of us know the theory of what to eat, yet still fall prey to all manner of poor eating habits.

4. **Constant worrying** is another way energy gets depleted. People often entertain fears and play out dramas in the mind, that never happen in real life. Not to mention carry the weight of the world on their shoulders. Imagine how much energy that takes?
5. **Inability to relax** is a major issue. There never seems to be enough time to re-fuel. Finding time to really rest and relax seems to be an alien concept in our fast-paced world.

So how about you, where are you now?

This is a simple exercise; you will need your journal and a pen. Note the date in your journal then take time to reflect on your life at this moment. Record your thoughts, feelings and motivations. Describe where you are now as clearly as you can. Below are some key questions to support you. Answer some or all of them in your journal or use the note pages provided.

- Where are you now in your body? How is your physical health and how are you maintaining and improving your health? What needs to change?

- Where are you now with your food choices? How is your diet? What needs to change?

- Where are you now in your mind and emotions? How is your psychological health? Do you respect your own thoughts and feelings?

- Where are you now spiritually? How is your spiritual health? Do you have a spiritual or religious orientation? Do you have a daily spiritual practice? What is emerging in your life now calling you to address your spirituality?

What is changing?

- Are you involved in work that you love? Do you have a vision of how you would like to work? What needs to change?

- What motivates you at the moment? What is unfolding in you? What is changing? Is there anything coming up for you that you really need to honor?

Reflect on what you have written. Appreciate where you are now and give thanks for the Divine blessing. It has taken time, energy and lots of life lessons to be exactly where you are. Don't be surprised by how well you are already doing, we often underestimate the progress we have already made. And if it doesn't look so good, still give thanks because everything is changing in this very moment. Take a breath and know that it's better to bring in the light than blame the darkness. So what are you committed to changing?

Where do you really want to be?

Let's start by acknowledging this statement from my first book *Opening to Spirit: "We must remember that the future is not a definite reality, which awaits us, it is for us to consciously create the future together."*

Every minute of every day you are not only living, you are also programming your destiny. Each thought programs your destiny. The food you eat, your attitude, the vibration and frequency you operate on, the people you meet and spend time with, all determine your future. Destiny is not a matter of chance, it is a matter of choice. What are you choosing for your life? Ask yourself and answer honestly, what is it you *really, really* want to be, do or have? What is it you dream of? What is the universe dreaming for you?

Expanding your Dreams

This is a visualization exercise. Take a moment in your minds-eye to expand on your dreams. Sitting in a relaxed and open posture close your eyes and ...

- Look inside with your inner eye. How do you look when your potential is fully expressed, where are you, how do you feel, what are you doing, who is in your life?

- How do you look when you are embracing your spiritual, emotional, physical and material wholeness? How does it feel? What has changed?

- Be still in this powerful place, drink in and enjoy the vibration, expand the vibration. Be you in all your wholeness, your greatness, *Be* vibrant and energy filled.

- Take a moment to note in your journal your thoughts, images and feelings. You can write or draw. The act of committing your dreams / visions / visualizations to paper can be very powerful. Note everything, even the wild stuff! It's all part of the creative process. This is how we bring things into being.

What do you dream of? Do you want a greater connection and understanding of the spirit that moves through you? Do you need to change the way you think? Many of us do, we need to be less afraid, more trusting and willing to recognize the beauty surrounding us every moment. It sounds good, but is it part of your dream? Could your health be better, is that what you see or is it money to buy the home of your dreams? Whatever it is dare to express it, dare to tell yourself. That way you welcome new energy into your life. Everything you dream of is energy. You have the ability to shape universal energy anyway you want.

Some of us are afraid to admit that we lack something deep inside, especially when what the world sees of us is the great job we have and material wealth. For others, our spirits soar yet we have no job, money or visible wealth.

Search your body, mind and soul, be honest with yourself. Thoughts have tremendous power and you are the co-creator of your destiny. Bring what you really want to be, do or have into your conscious awareness today. Admit it to yourself today, write it down today and start creating your dream life today. Tomorrow's Reality Undoubtedly Starts Today – TRUST.

Presence and Gratitude

Energy is flowing and awareness is growing as you develop a greater sense of where you are now and where you want to be.

"We often treat life as if it is a problem we need to solve, rather than a wonder unfolding for us to enjoy"[1]

Life is a journey of unfolding and becoming. Where you are now is perfect in its imperfection. Give thanks for all that has unfolded in your life this far bringing you to where you are now. Adopt an attitude of presence and gratitude.

As you enter the presence of now, as you still yourself in any moment on your sacred life journey, as you embrace the emptiness of now, the richness of this instant, know that in this very moment nothing is lacking, all is well in this moment.

"Tomorrow's a mystery, yesterday history, today a gift and that is why we give thanks and call it the present."

The ability to be present in every moment and give thanks for the breath we breathe is to be rich. Know that all we really ever have is the moment. And being present in each moment offers the greatest gift of life. It is when we are able to give thanks for the small things in life that we open to greater abundance.

Throughout time it has been recognised that to obtain more from the universe we need to give thanks for what we already have and stay open to spirit. Incorporating energy exercises, rest and relaxation into your daily life along with positive thoughts and actions, allows more energy to flow freely through your system, blessing you abundantly. This also increases your level of well-being, effectiveness and fulfilment in life.

Earlier we took a new look at the ancient chakra system seeing how life is an ever evolving journey of consciousness taking us from the Newtonian material world of manifestation and success right through to the resting place of non-dual consciousness where the created rests in the arms of the Creator becoming one. The beauty of the Chakra system and its seven stages of consciousness is that it allows us to bring together the Newtonian worldview and the newer quantum worldview and practically apply both in an integral way of life. This transforms the way we live.

The conclusion of this book is creating an action plan. A programme of activities to incorporate in everyday life that brings increased energy, vitality, consciousness and a greater quality of life. So as you become present and give thanks, allow the energy and inner intelligence moving through you, to reveal the changes you are ready to commit to.

Creating your Desired Transformation

E4L is all about creating lasting change and transforming lives. It's about embracing health, happiness, success and fulfilment. It's about balancing our worldly needs, after all we do still live on earth, with our spiritual desire to elevate consciousness and become one with the Creator. E4L is a way of achieving high energy conscious living. Let me share one of my favourite quotes by Will Rogers:

> *"Even if you are on the right track you will get run over if you just sit there."*

Sounds funny, but how many of us learn the theory get on the right track and then do nothing to embody change. This time let's make it different.

Energy 4 Life invites you to:

- Choose what you want to change
- Choose what is realistic for you to do each day
- Honor your spirit while living in the world
- Embrace what brings you greater, health, happiness, success and fulfilment
- Live a high energy conscious life

This is a good time to look in your journal and revisit your values. Who and what is important to you? How can you raise your energy levels and live more consciously?

You have four modalities to choose from:

1. **Energy Exercises** to re-energise your body and increase the quantity of your energy
2. **Energy Psychology** to release stress, free your mind and improve the quality of your energy
3. **Energy Foods** that re-vitalize your system and raise the vibration of your energy
4. **Energy Balance** to relax, calm and elevate the frequency of your energy

There are three types of people in the world, those who make things happen, those who let things happen and those who wonder what happened!

So why not make things happen and enhance your energy levels by developing your own high energy action programme.

High Energy Action Programme

A high energy action programme is a commitment to yourself.

It's an agreement that details the steps you are going to take to achieve your desired transformation. Your programme should be positive and encouraging. It can include easily achievable tasks as well as more challenging ones.

Lifelines[2] should be incorporated and details of the support you need. Action programmes are designed to move you from where you are now to where you want to be. Writing your programme and detailing individual activities helps clarify what needs to be done and makes the process of change less overwhelming. A good programme inspires you to take action and also evaluates your progress.

A good high energy action programme:

- Inspires you to action
- Details your activities with relevant dates and lifelines
- Records your achievements and progress

It's good to commit to daily practices, weekly, monthly and annual activities that support your values and desire for high energy conscious living:

Consider:

- Creating a daily power half hour of Energy Exercises and Energy Balance. Make any daily dietary adjustments.
- Creating a longer weekly session with your favourite E4L practices. Journal work, meditation, relaxation all the things you find energizing and uplifting.
- Receiving a monthly E4L maintenance session with one of our practitioners or coaches. If there isn't one in your area, consider training yourself.
- Attending an E4L retreat at least once a year where you can Re-charge your energy and Take-charge of your life.

List all the Energy 4 Life practices you could incorporate into your Life.

1 ______________________________

2 ______________________________

3 ______________________________

4 ______________________________

5 ______________________________

6 ______________________________

7 ______________________________

Answer the questions below to clarify what you are willing to commit to.

Daily I could

____

____

____

____

____

____

Weekly I could

Monthly I could

Yearly I could

Revisit your positive affirmation which I invited you to create in the chapter on Energy Psychology and your vision/dream from this chapter. You can use them as part of your action programme. Below is a simple outline for your action programme or get creative and design your own. Write your name on the dotted line and fill in the gaps using the information you have gathered and practices you are committed to.

....High Energy Action Programme

Date: ....

My Achievements so far

1.
2.
3.
4.
5.

My Vision:

My Top Three Values:

1.
2.
3.

Affirmation and positive new Life Script

Energy Exercises I commit to

1.
2.
3.
4.
5.

Energy Food changes I commit to

1.
2.
3.

Energy Balance practices I embrace

1.
2.
3.

Actions and start dates.

Daily I will

____

____

____

____________________ Starting on....................................

Weekly I will

____

____

____

____________________ Starting on....................................

Monthly I will

____

____

____

____________________ Starting on....................................

My annual energy renewal is

____

____

____

____________________ Starting on....................................

"An Aspect of your destiny is redefined each day."

Now you have an action programme for utilizing E4L everyday creating dharma, a dedicated way of life. E4L will become a daily ritual and opportunity to elevate energy. Before we come to the end of this book, let me take a moment to summarize by sharing ten principles of E4L and conclude with seven secrets that support high energy conscious living.

High Energy Conscious Living.

E4L is a natural health care system and conscious living programme that works with the Chakras and HES to create health, happiness and success. Transformative tools and techniques are used to raise the quantity, quality, frequency and vibration of your energy.

Ten Principles of Energy 4 Life

1. **Energy is the conscious animating force behind all life.** It changes form but cannot be destroyed. (Just as H_2O changes from water to steam or ice).

2. **Free flowing energy is essential for health and wellbeing.** Uninterrupted energy flows in a constant rhythm of Expansion and Contraction through the body-mind spirit continuum.

3. **Energy is the fuel humans are designed to function on.** We need regularly topped up, good quality, high vibration, high frequency energy for optimum health and wellbeing.

4. **Energy is the matrix connecting all aspects of life.** E4L uses an integral approach raising awareness of how you use or abuse personal energy resources in all areas of life.

E4L coaches you towards energy mastery helping you develop health, happiness, success and fulfilment. E4L invites you to create a high energy action programme.

5. **Don't wait to get ill before taking care of your life.** E4L advocates energy education for all the family, providing restorative practices and easy to use energy techniques that can be used by children at home and at school and adults at home and at work. E4L is designed to enhance health and help you avoid stress and illness forever.

E4L offers:
Healing & Restoration it can be used to return the body to optimum health.
Maintenance & Prevention ensuring that the body stays healthy.
Enhanced Health of body, mind and spirit.

6. **E4L is an integral approach addressing physical health, psych-emotional stability and spiritual development.**
I have always been a generalist and have chosen to research and practice numerous systems that pertain to our overall wellbeing. E4L draws on and creates a powerful synthesis of all the following:

- Art and Science of Yoga
- Humanistic Psychology
- Naturopathy
- Energy based Somatic Therapies
- Ancient Spiritual Traditions
- New Paradigm Medicine
- Quantum Physics and Consciousness Studies
- Personal Coaching

From my experience of working with these systems, I utilized the most potent, quick acting, powerful techniques and created E4L. Very early on I realized that underlying everything is the flow of energy. Therefore the two main questions in E4L are:

1. How do you use or abuse your energy?
2. How could you use it better?

7. **Life is all about energy and how you manage it**. When you understand this paradigm and learn tools and skills for managing energy – your vital life force, you will always have all the energy for life you need.

   E4L skills are synthesized into four main modalities relating to four elements.

• Energy Exercises	re-energize your body	Earth
• Energy Psychology	releases stress and frees the mind	Air
• Energy Foods	re-vitalize your system	Fire
• Energy Balance	relaxes and calms	Water

Getting to grips with how we use or abuse personal energy is essential for healthy and successful living. E4L provides an alternative way to view and cope with life. How are you using or abusing your energy and how could you use it better, is the main question?

Many people have had the experience of seeing a therapist, doctor or psychotherapist, dealing with problems only to find they return. This happens because they have not dealt with the energy level. As energy creates a matrix and template, if nothing changes at the energy level, following the old energetic template problems are easily re-created. E4L gets to the CORE and effects change on the energetic level.

8. **Metaphor is the language of Energy.** We all describe our

energy in different ways. We may speak of *feeling full of energy* or *low in energy,* being *in good spirits* or *having no energy*. We may feel high, light, open, we know something good will happen or we can feel heavy, drained, weight on our shoulders, stabbed in the back etc. The language of energy allows us to communicate our inner landscape. E-motions are Movements of Energy.

These core statements are feedback devices that tell us what is happening on an energy level. We may not be able to see, hear or measure the energy system but we do experience it and this we share in the language of metaphor.

9. **Energy 4 Life offers a paradigm shift** and the opportunity to change your life and coach others to change theirs. Implement these skills for managing energy and you will always have all the energy for life you need.

10. **Energy. Your life depends on it.** It is key to a high quality of life

Seven Secrets that support High Energy Conscious Living

1. If you are not creating EASE in your life you are creating dis-ease
2. Quit struggling and celebrate being whoever and wherever you are
3. Increase your awareness daily of what's really important to you
4. Own up to your weaknesses but focus on your strengths
5. Have more time – start your day 30 minutes early with a power half hour
6. Stop and relax for at least two minutes in every hour
7. Enjoy the journey – this moment is all you really have

Practice something from E4L everyday and say yes to health, happiness, success and fulfilment. Having abundant energy and vitality is a lifestyle choice. Embrace High Energy Conscious Living and make the rest of your life the best of your life and make our world a better place one person at a time.

Glossary

Describes the meaning of terminology used in this book.

Akasha: space or ether, the infinite possibility that gives rise to all life.

Akashic Field: primordial container and source of energy and information. Like an original cyberspace.

Akashic Record: information of all that was, is and shall be contained in the Ether.

Ancient Chakra System: the original Chakra system consisting of 7 major chakras, 21 minor chakras, 49 minute chakras and numerous vortices of energy where nadis cross over.

Chakra: energy vortices in the body with direct links to the neuro-endocrine system.

Dharma: right livelihood, living life according to your soul purpose.

Energy System: consists of energy, energy pathways, the aura and energy field.

Energy Field: Subtle, vibrating force that flows through and around the body.

Embodiment: to fully experience and be present in the physical body.

Energy Crisis: occurs when demand on personal energy resources exceeds supply.

Energy Signature: your unique energetic identity, a specific pattern of energy.

Enlightenment: to know and experience life from a place of spiritual elevation.

Evolution: the ever unfolding journey and return of all things from matter to spirit.

Guna: quality of consciousness and specific energetic frequency.

Human Energy System (HES): consists of energy, energy

pathways, the aura and energy field.

Human Potential Movement: emerged in the 1960s along with Humanistic Psychology. The core beliefs are that all humans have infinite potential that can be developed and fully expressed.

Involution: - the movement of all things from pure spirit into gross physical matter on the earthly plane.

Koshas: five subtle sheaths or layers - physical, energetic, emotional, cognitive and spiritual.

Laser Question: coaching question that hones in on one specific area or issue.

Lifeline: time limit. Acknowledgment of life and something new created rather than a deadline.

Nadi: Sanskrit term for 72.000 pathways in and around the body where energy flows.

Nirvana: Buddhist concept meaning blissful. Consciousness beyond the cycle of life and death.

Non-dual: the experience and recognition of oneness. All is One.

Ongoing Evolutionary Process (OEP): the force driving the continuous journey of life as it unfolds.

Peak Experience: heightened state of consciousness, term used by A. Maslow.

Prana: Sanskrit for energy, breath, life force.

Quantum Vacuum: is an 'empty space' which according to quantum field theory is full of potential particles.

Samadhi: concept from yoga and Vedanta philosophy, blissful level of consciousness and spiritual liberation. (There are several levels of Samadhi).

Soul Purpose: life path that resonates on a very deep level, as if destined before birth.

Startle Wastes: excess neuro-chemicals caused by stress.

Theory of Everything (TOE): in physics this relates to a theory that can explain and link together all known physical phenomena.

Transpersonal: beyond the personal, relating to spiritual, universal levels of experience.

Unity Consciousness: my definition is the coming together of the very best wisdom teachings from three sources, ancient tradition, religion and modern science. This creates a powerful synergy that can propel us to a higher level of spirit infused consciousness. It is also the recognition and acknowledgement of unity in all things.

References

Chapter One

1. $E= mc^2$ defined. E is Energy - M is Mass - C is the speed of light - 2 is squared (to the 2nd power) and refers to C. Mass can be converted into energy, like an atomic power plant or bomb. $E= mc^2$ means energy has mass and mass has energy. A literal translation would be Energy=mass multiplied by the speed of light squared. Because the speed of light is a very large number and is multiplied by itself, this equation points out how a small amount of matter can release a huge amount of energy.
2. Wikipedia http://en.wikipedia.org/wiki/Energy
3. For a free seven day e-course on Creating EASE in your life and work, visit www.shola.co.uk and sign up for the Spirit of Success Newsletter.

Chapter Three

1. Andrew Newberg MD and Eugene D'Aquili PhD. *Why God won't go away* (Ballantine Books 2001)
2. Andrew Newberg MD and Eugene D'Aquili PhD. *Why God won't go away* (Ballantine Books 2001)
3. I use the term Evolutionary Psychology, to refer to the evolution of our psychological needs.
4. Neurones are found in the gut, making gut feeling yet another aspect of our intelligence.

Chapter Four

1. I explain more on this in my first book, *Opening to Spirit*. Where I explore the original Dravidian Tantric teachings and the later Aryan celibate teachings
2. The Yoruba from West Africa have a rich spiritual tradition that is popular in America and Latin America today. The

Author is of Nigeria, Yoruba parentage.
3. Caroline Shola Arewa *Opening to Spirit* (Thorson's UK 98)
4. Diane Witt, assistant professor of psychology New York
5. Gaia Vince *Scientists reveal the secret of cuddles*. (New scientist July 2002.) Original research by Associate Professor Håkan Olausson The journal, Nature Neuroscience.

Chapter Five

1. For more on the elements read my in-depth Chakra book. *Opening to Spirit*, available from www.shola.co.uk
2. Robert A. Charman *Complementary Therapies for Physical Therapists: A Theoretical and Clinical Exploration*. James Oschman is a contributor (Elsevier Health Sciences, 2000)

Chapter Six

1. Permission was given to use this case study. Names have been changed
2. For a more complete Values Elicitation Test. go to http://www.douglaswagoner.com/ValueTest.php
3. Heartmath institute has conducted extensive research. HeartMath is engaged in psychophysiology, neurocardiology and biophysics research. This research has significantly advanced the understanding of heart-brain interactions, heart-rhythm-pattern and heart-rate-variability analyses, emotional physiology and the physiology of optimal learning and performance. http://www.heartmath.org/
4. Eckhart Tolle *The Power of Now* (New world Library 2004)
5. © 2008 The Energy Release Technique ERT created by Caroline Shola Arewa, as part of the Energy 4 Life, Health and Conscious Living Programme
6. Dr Michael Beckwith Spiritual Leader and founder of Agape International Spiritual Community. Featured speaker on *The Secret* and Author of *Spiritual Liberation*. More information visit: www.agapelive.com

Chapter Seven

1. For more details on fasting, refer to Caroline Shola Arewa *Opening to Spirit* (Thorsons UK 98)
2. Spirulina and some other sea vegetables are sources of B12. However vegans and raw foodists are advised to test B12 levels in the body and supplement if necessary. Deficiency negatively affects the nervous system and is particularly important for pregnant women.

Chapter Eight

1. Ley lines form a grid on the earth's surface. Various places on the grid create vortices of energy, hotspots, where sacred sites and places of worship are often found such as in Glastonbury, Sedona, Mount Meru in Tanzania, Oshogbo in Nigeria.

Chapter Nine

1. Quoting Caroline Shola Arewa from *Opening to Spirit* (Thorsons UK 98)
2. I use the word lifeline instead of deadline. This focuses on what is being born and coming to life. When we reach our lifelines we gain new life. Even if it relates to something we didn't want to do, when we reach the lifeline, we will get our life back.

About the Author

Shola is a humanistic psychologist, master of yoga and author of four books including the highly acclaimed *Opening to Spirit*.

Shola is known as the *Energy Doctor,* for her pioneering and award winning work with core energy and the chakra system. She is committed to elevating energy, evolving consciousness and improving our world. For over 25 years she has supported people to balance energy and transform their lives. As a leading light in spiritual and personal development she helps people reinstate health, in body, mind and spirit.

Shola trained practitioners in complementary medicine for 10 years, winning a CAM Award in 2008. An international speaker and workshop presenter recognised for her gentle yet powerful style always infused with knowledge, creativity and laughter.

Shola is passionate about the spiritual revolution we are now experiencing and is a Spiritual Coaching Trainer and created the popular ***Energy 4 Life*** conscious living programme. She has presented seminars on every continent and appeared on radio and TV worldwide.

Resources

If you would like to know more about **Energy 4 Life** and are interested in changing your life and supporting others to change theirs, please contact shola@energy-4life.com for a full Energy 4 Life training brochure.

For information on consultations, workshops and retreats please visit www.energy-4life.com

To book Shola for talks and workshops at your event visit, www.shola.co.uk

For a free 7 day e-course, Spirit of Success newsletter and information on other books by Shola visit www.shola.co.uk

Personal Notes

Personal Notes

Personal Notes